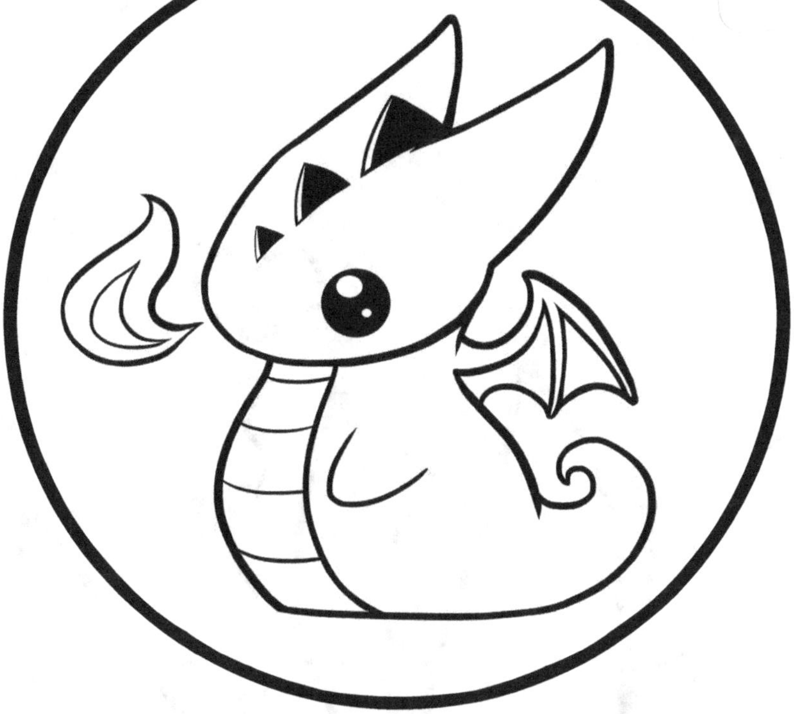

COLOR
Dragons and Beasties

Illustrated by Becca Golins

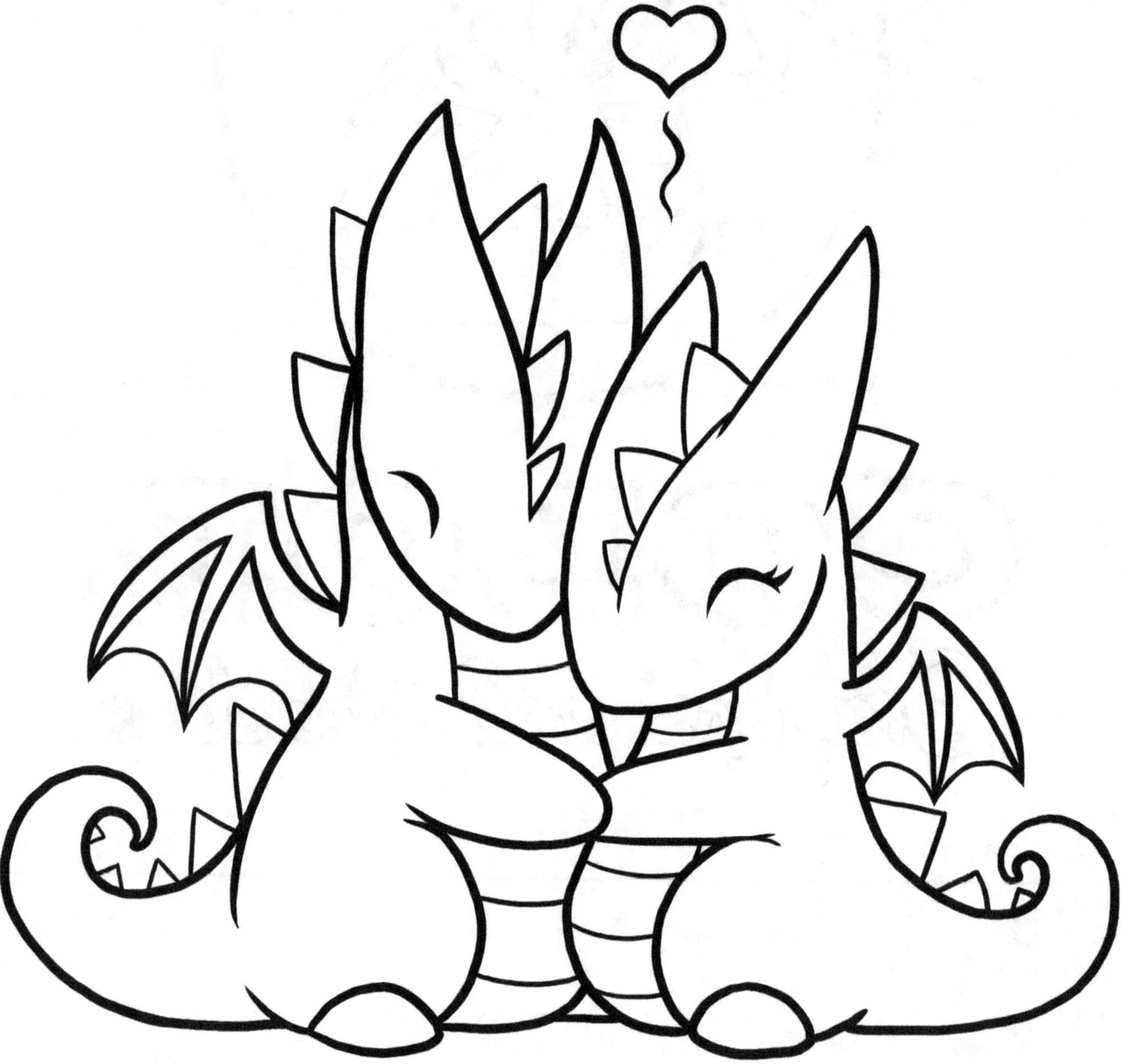

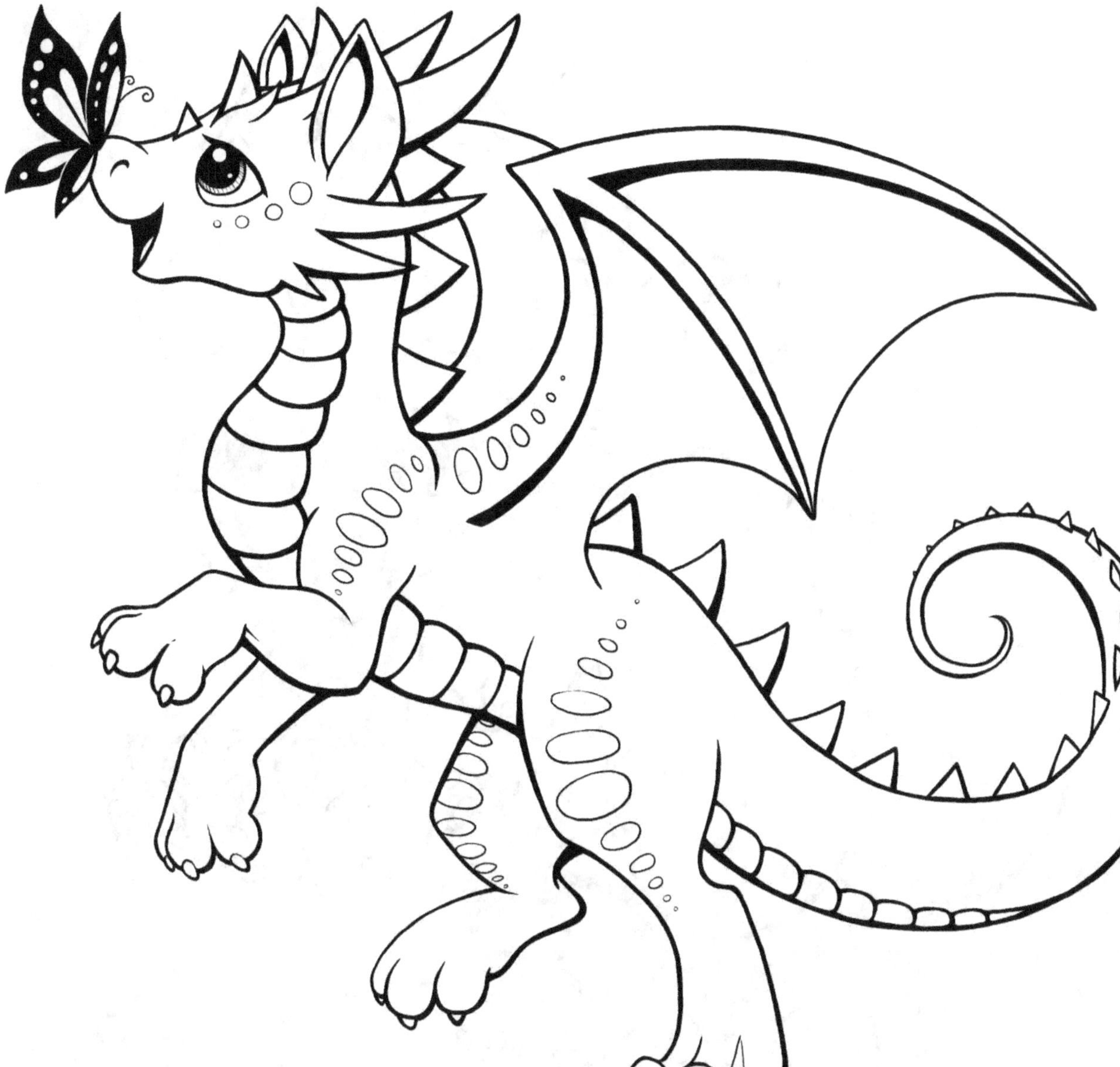

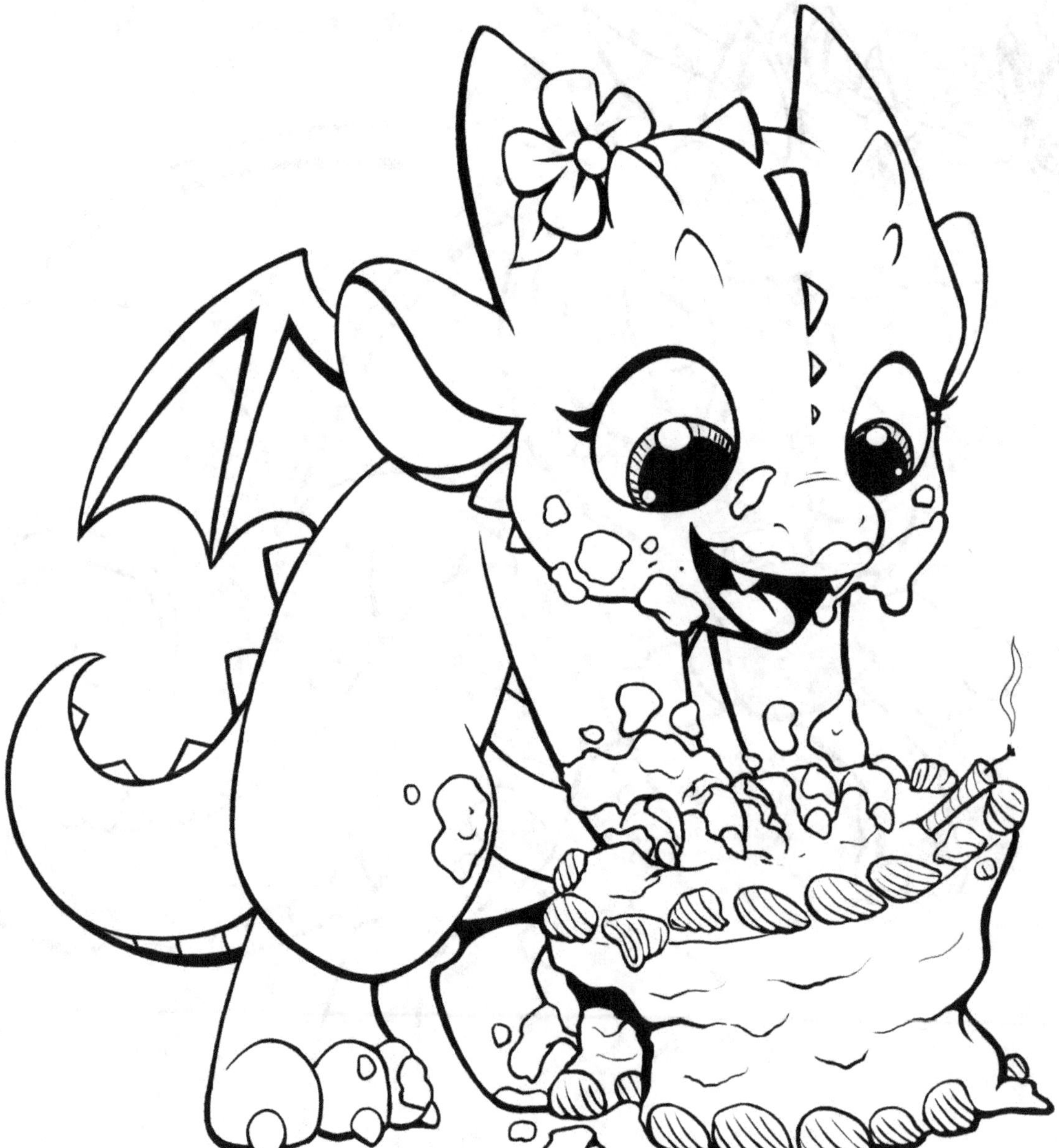

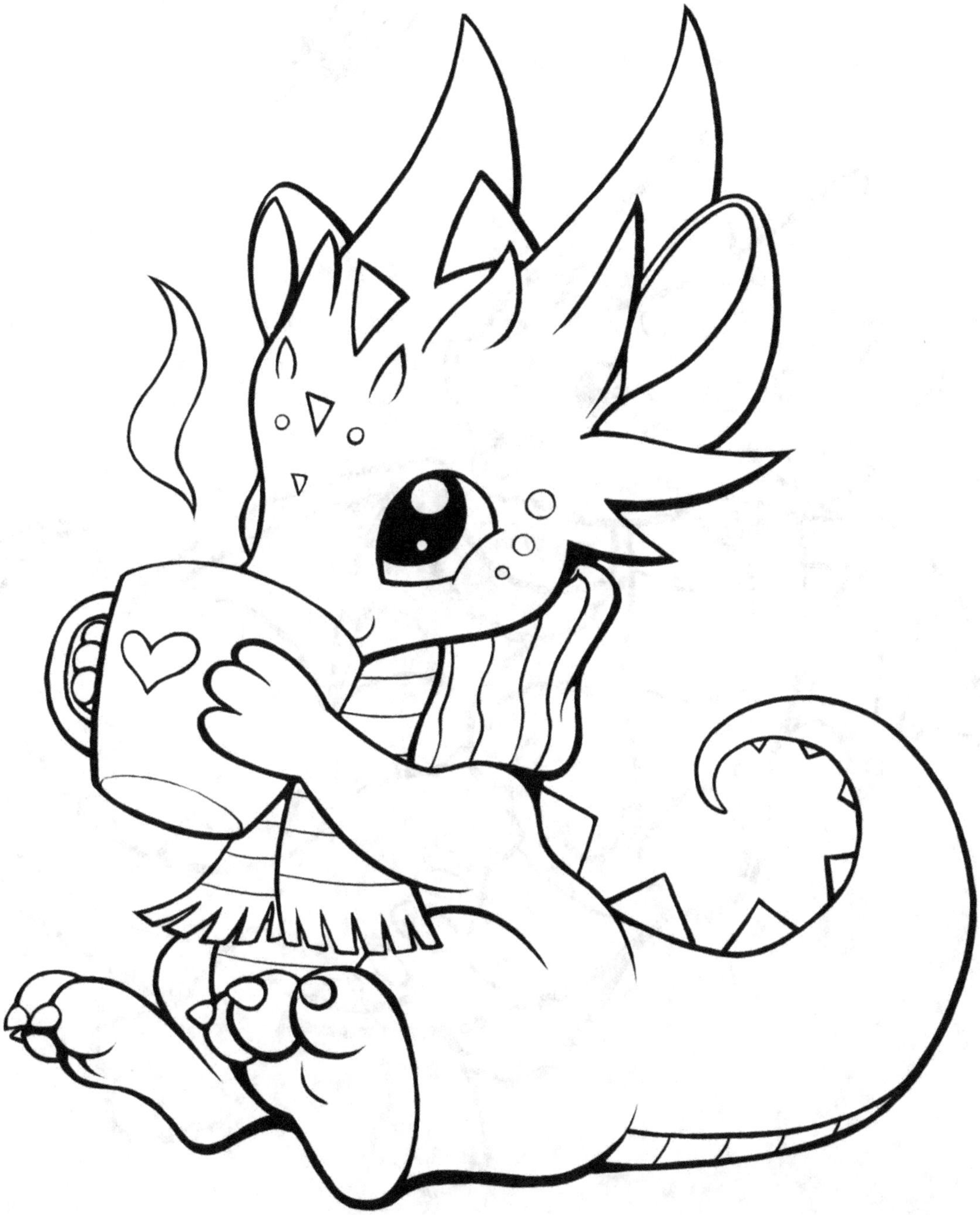

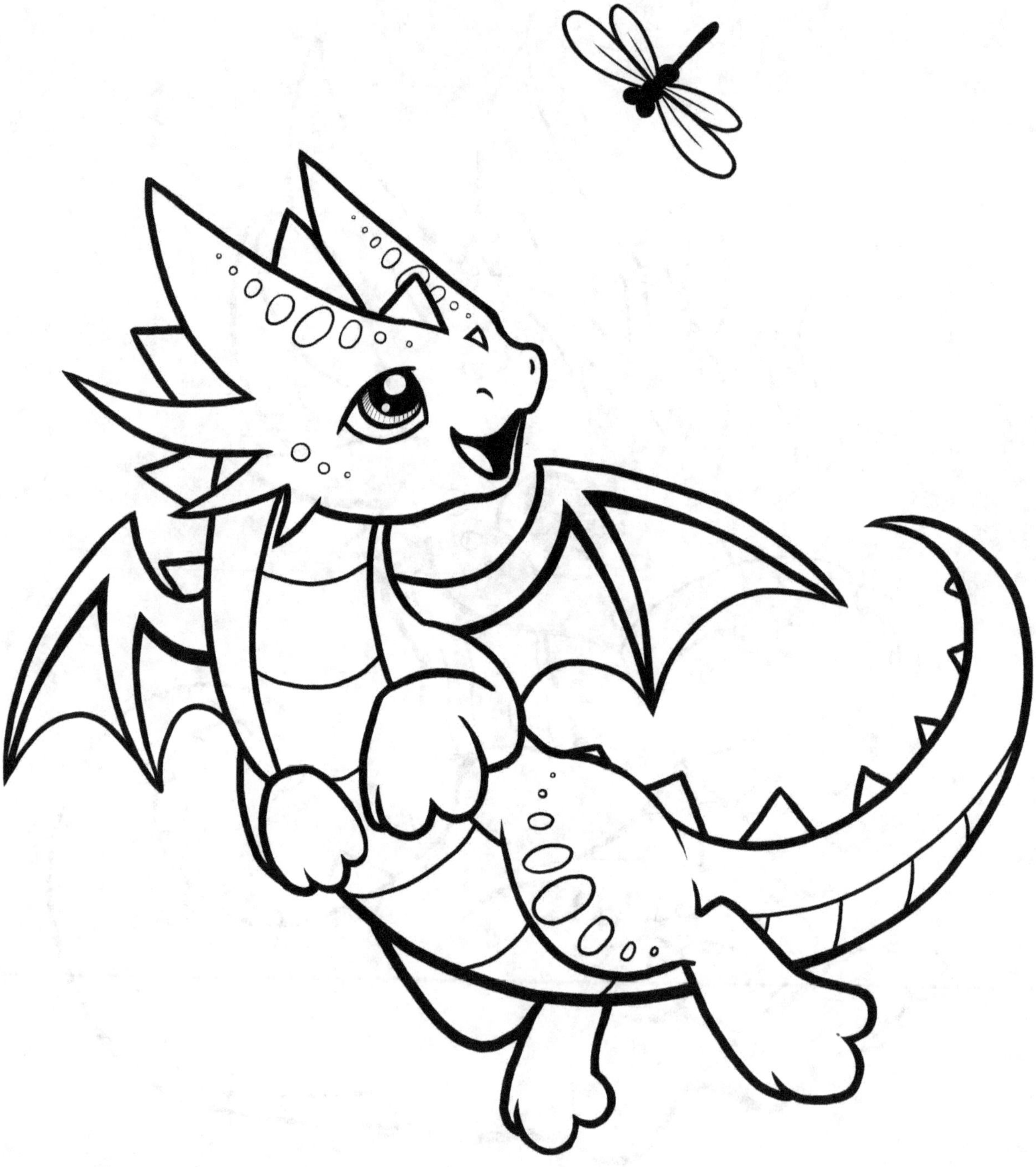

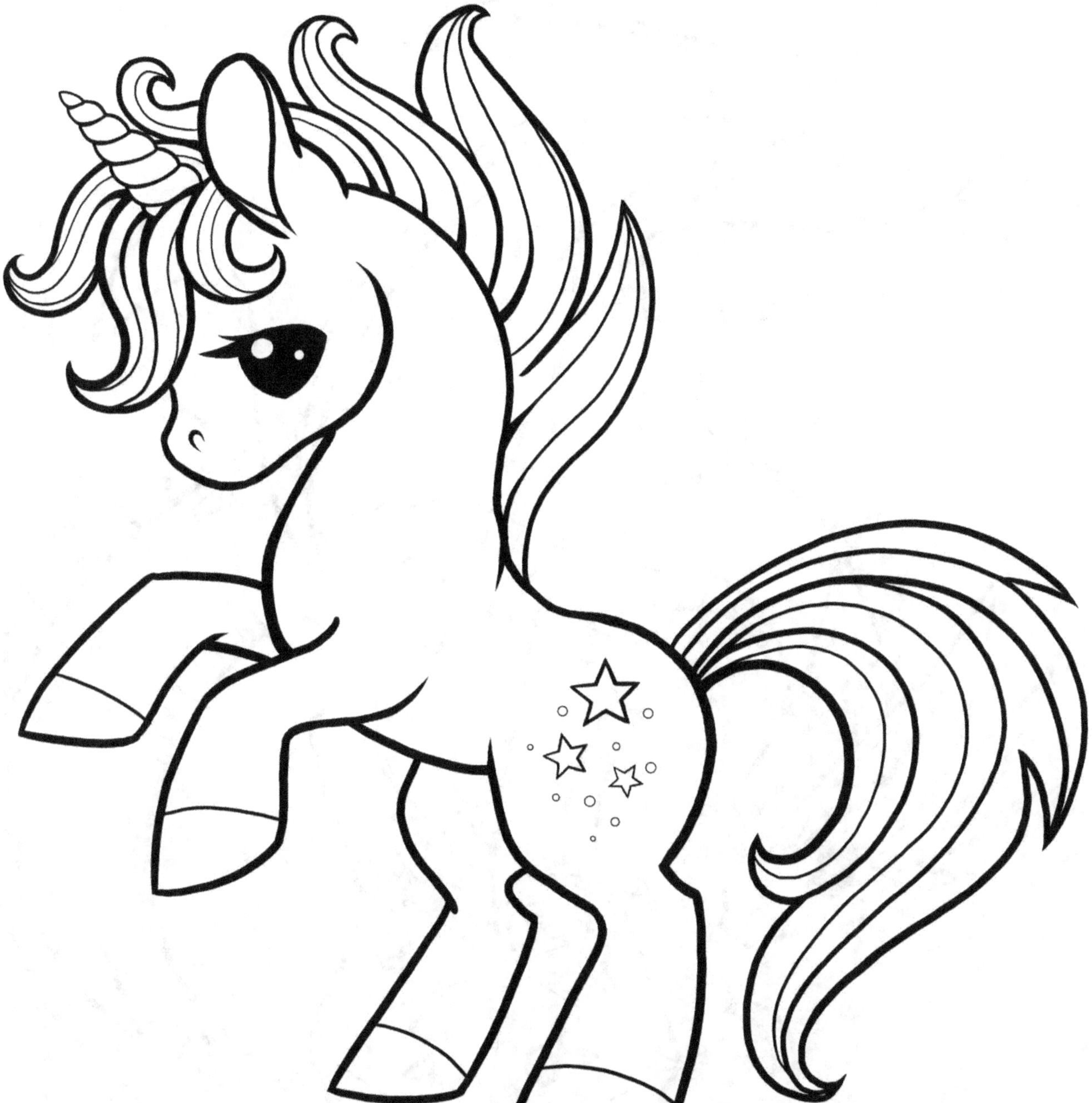

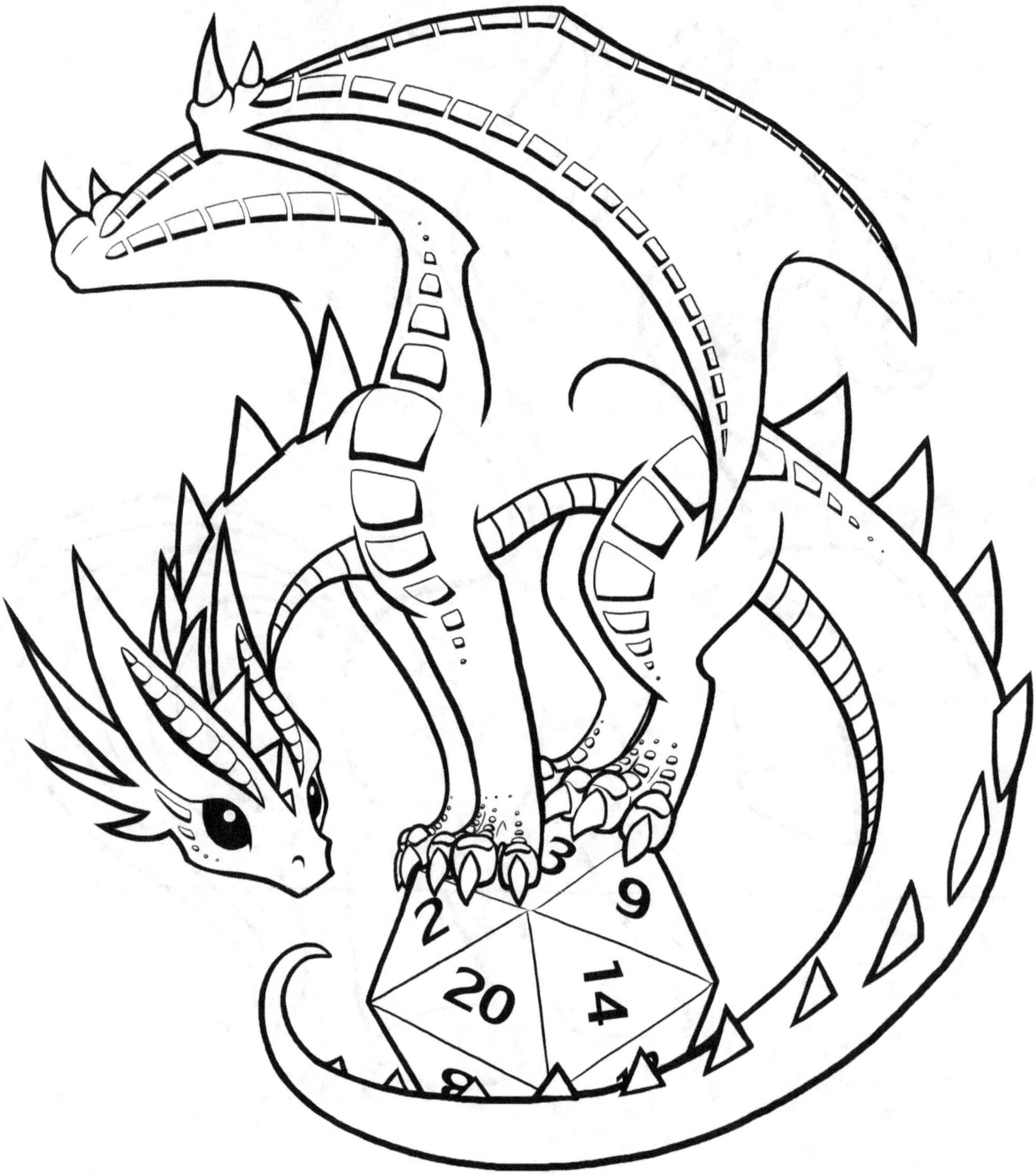
3
9
2
20
14

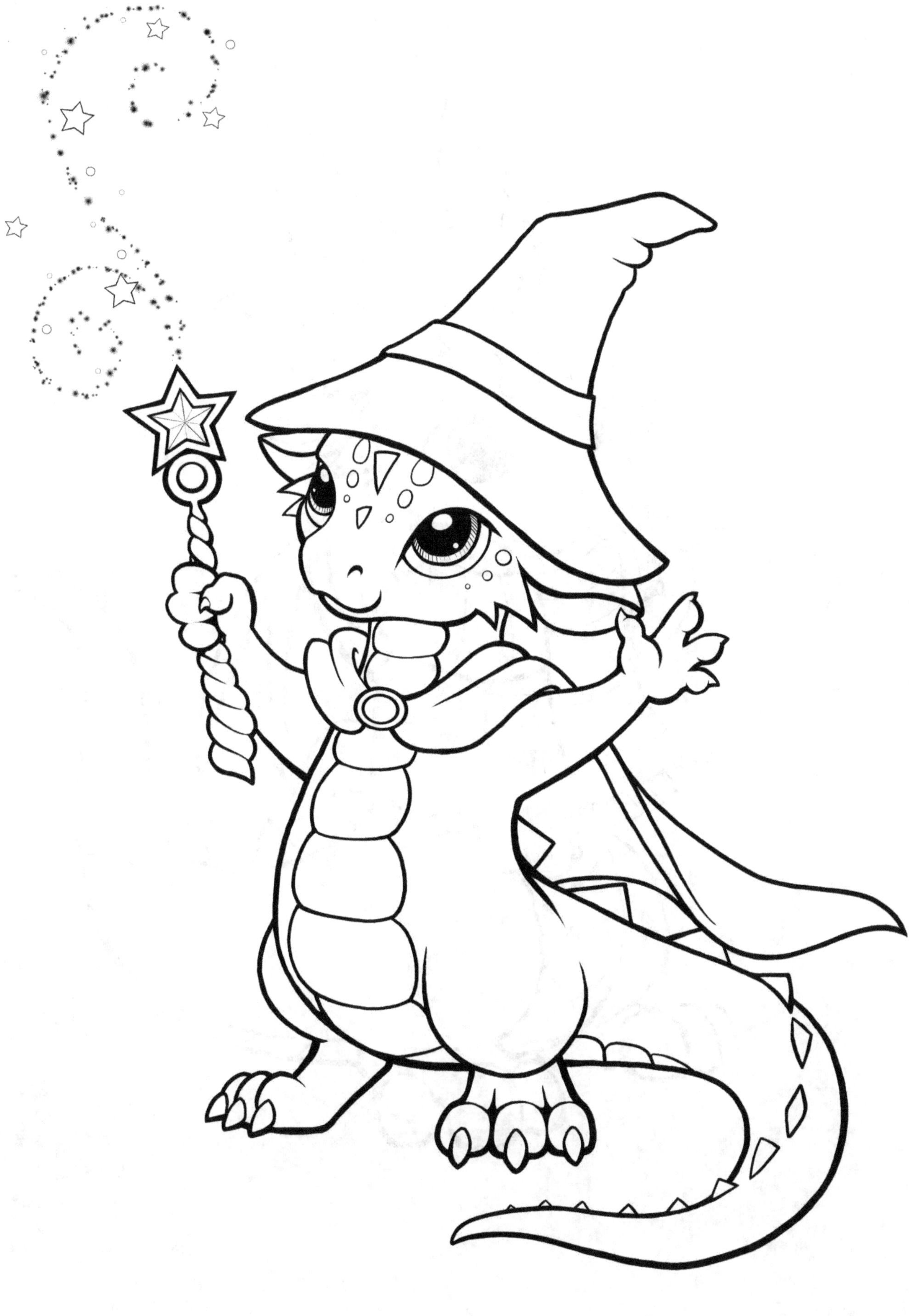

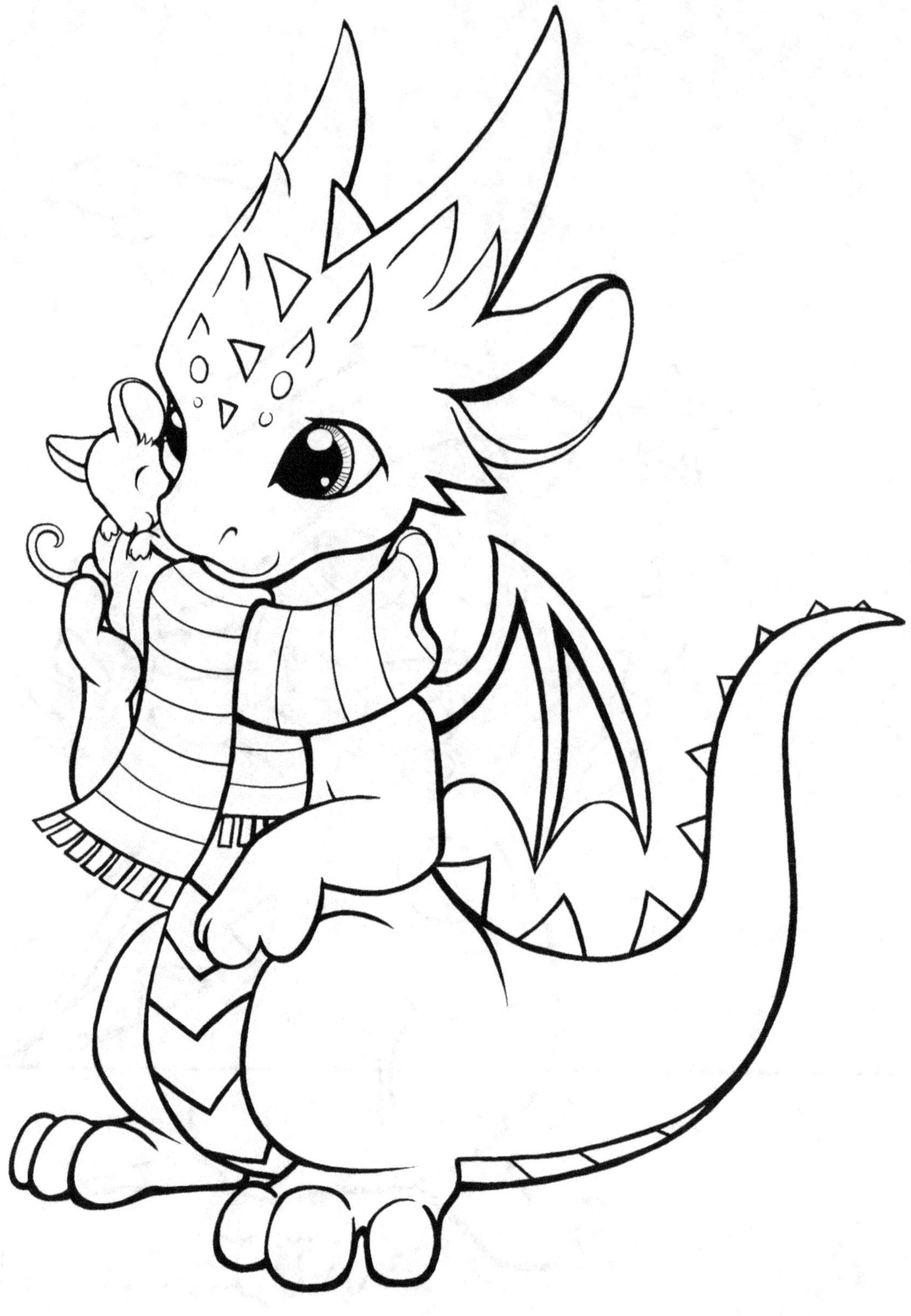

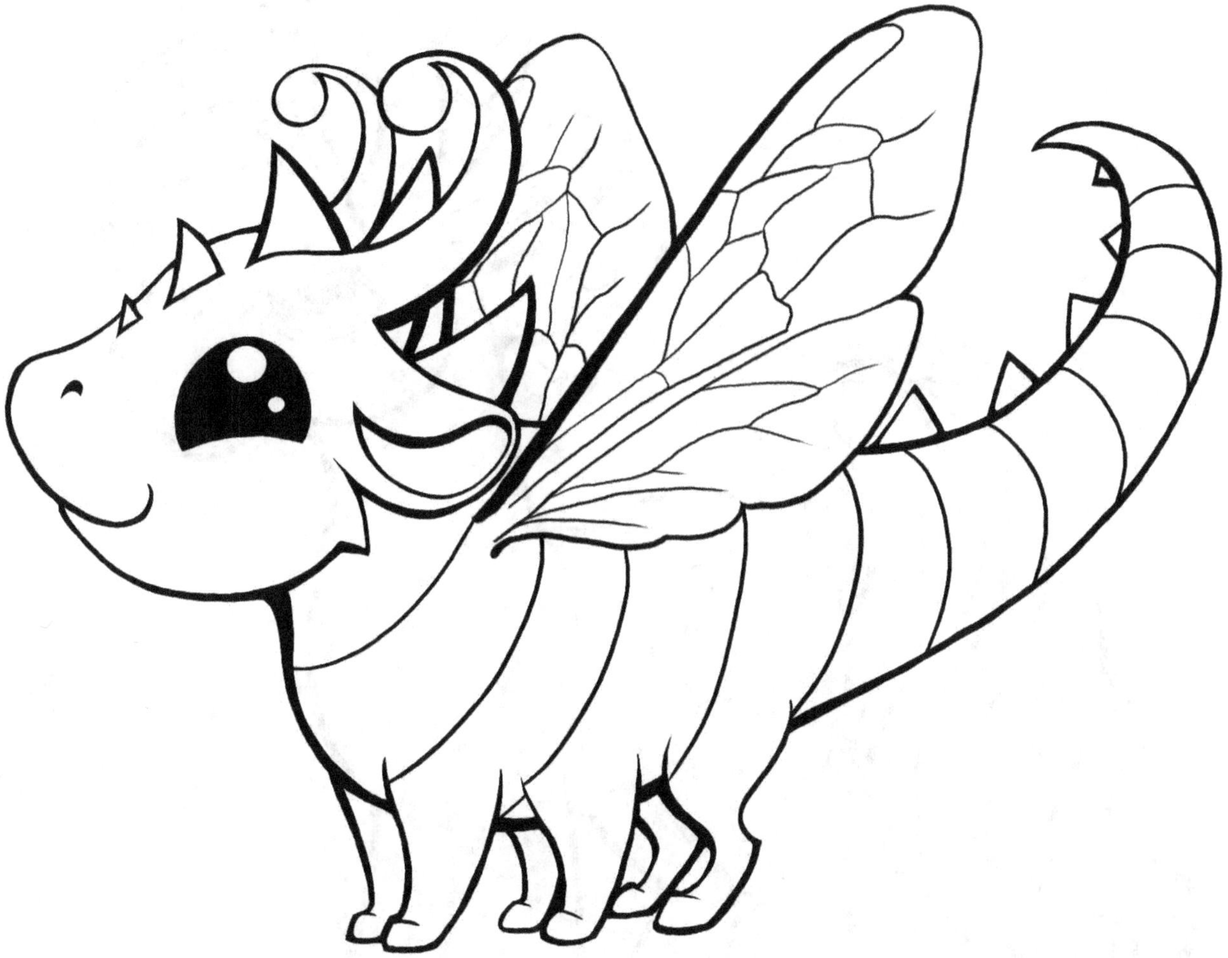

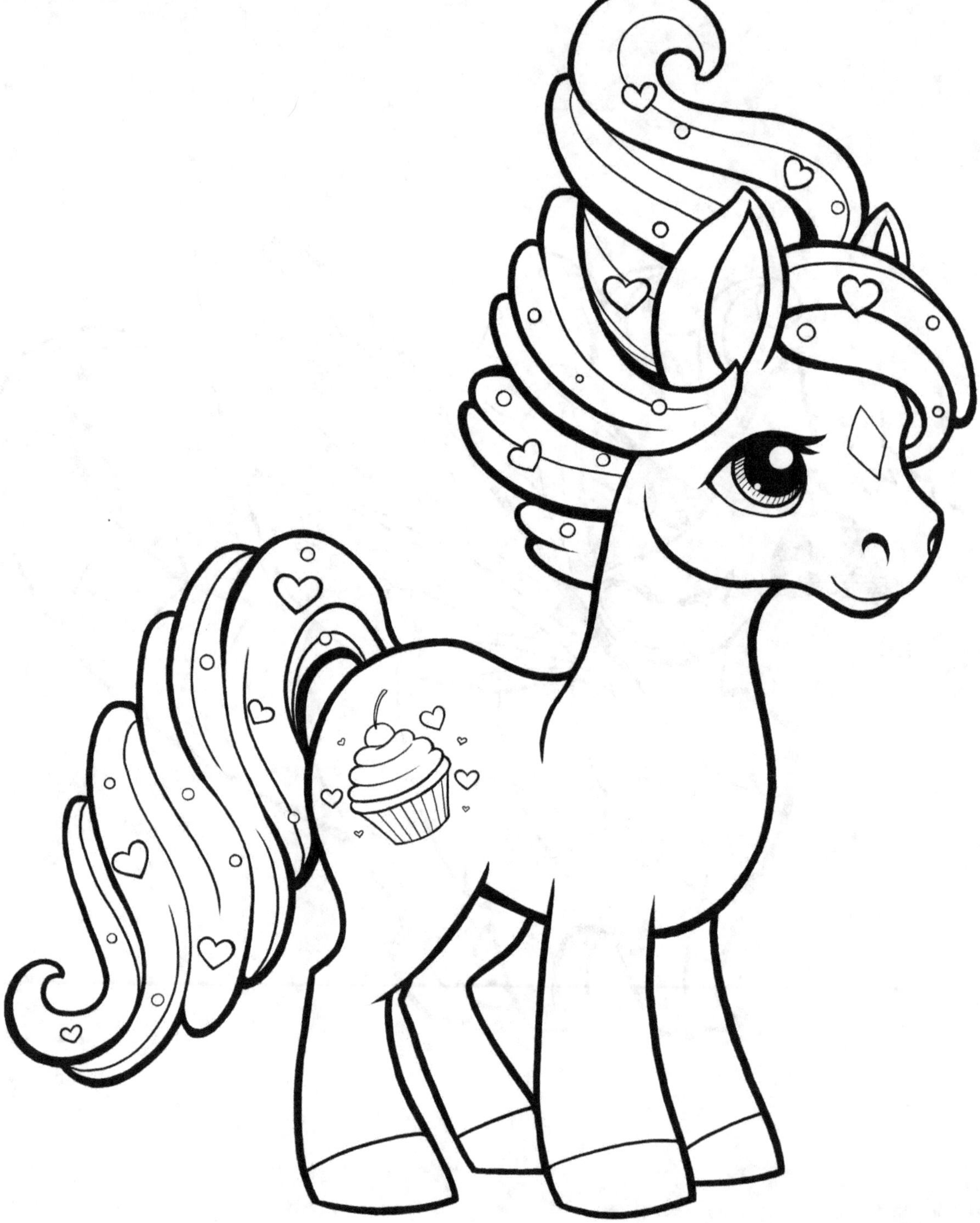

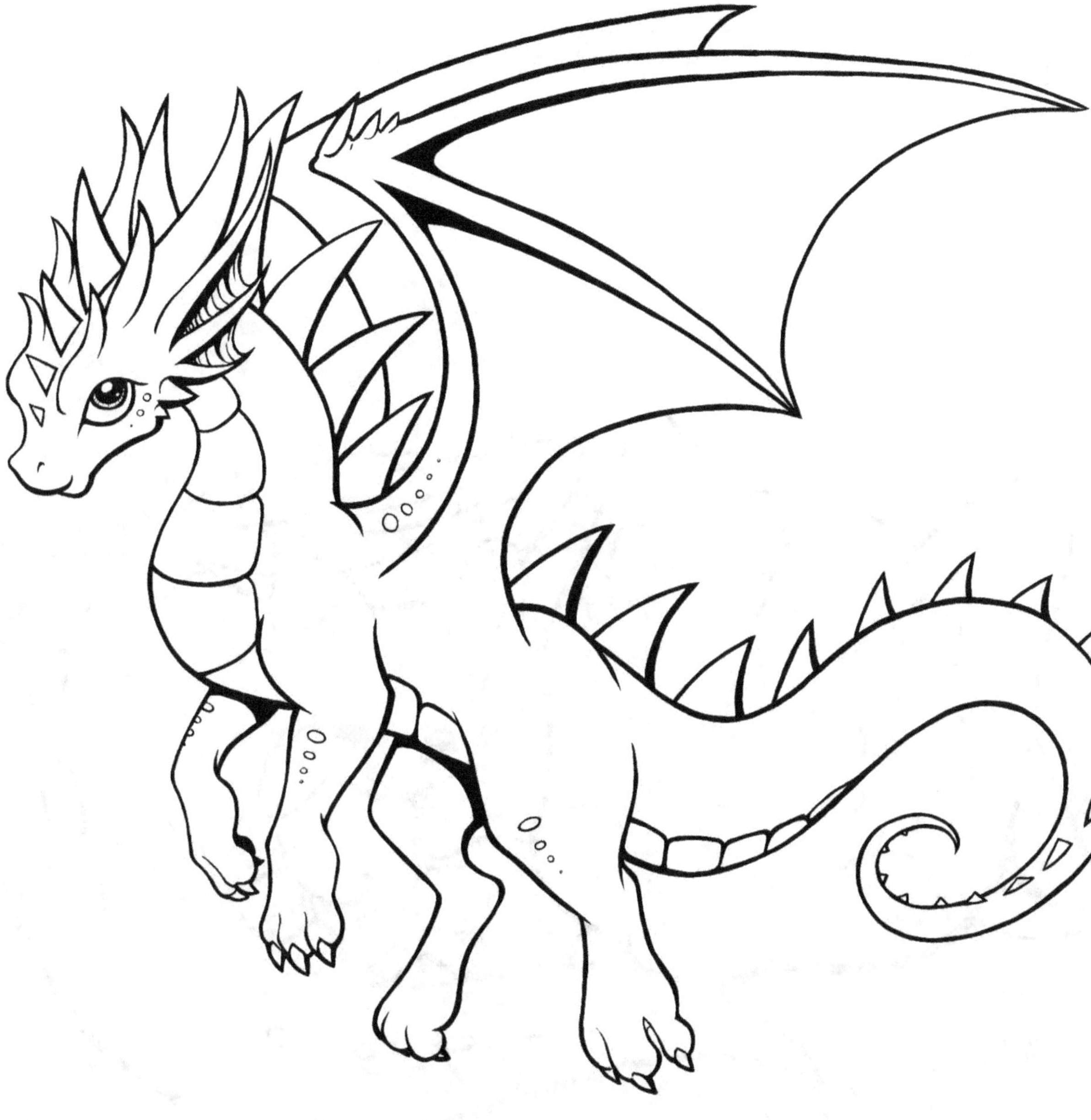

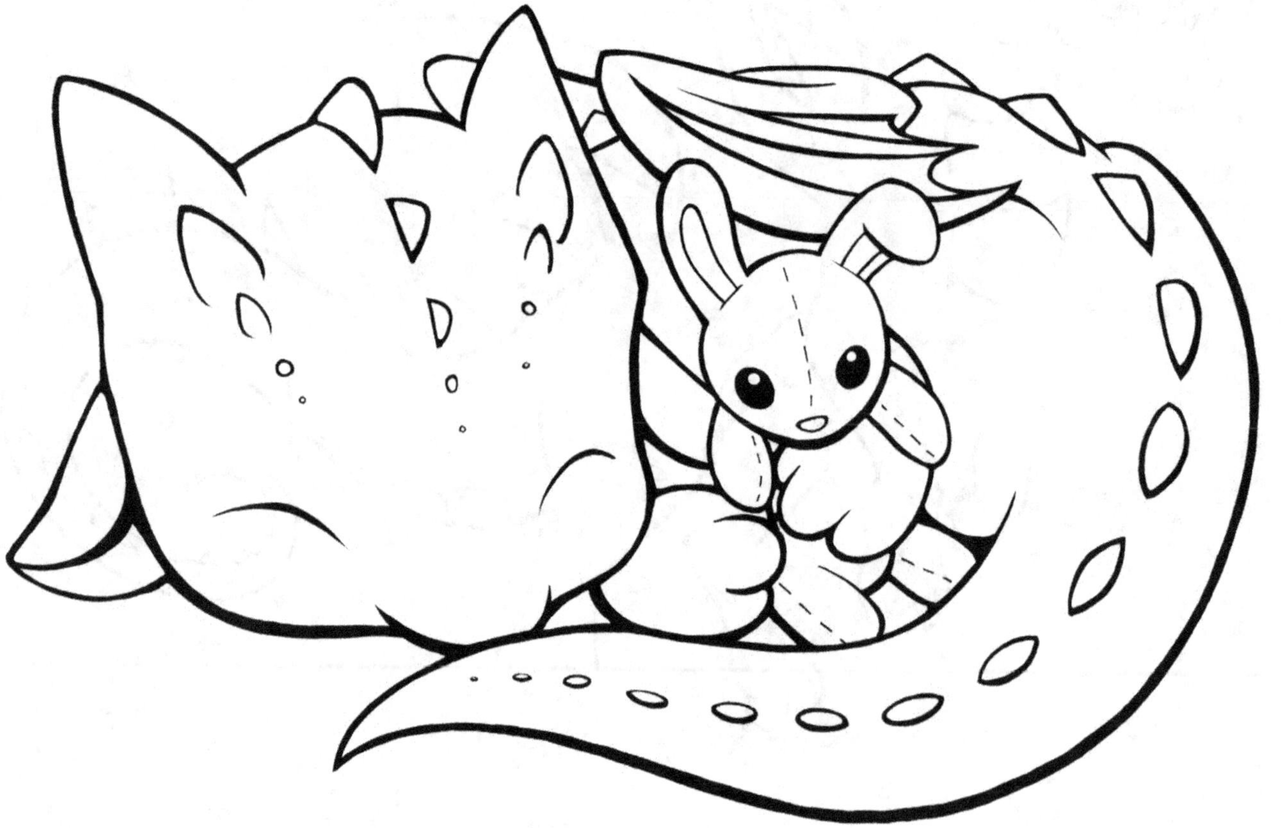

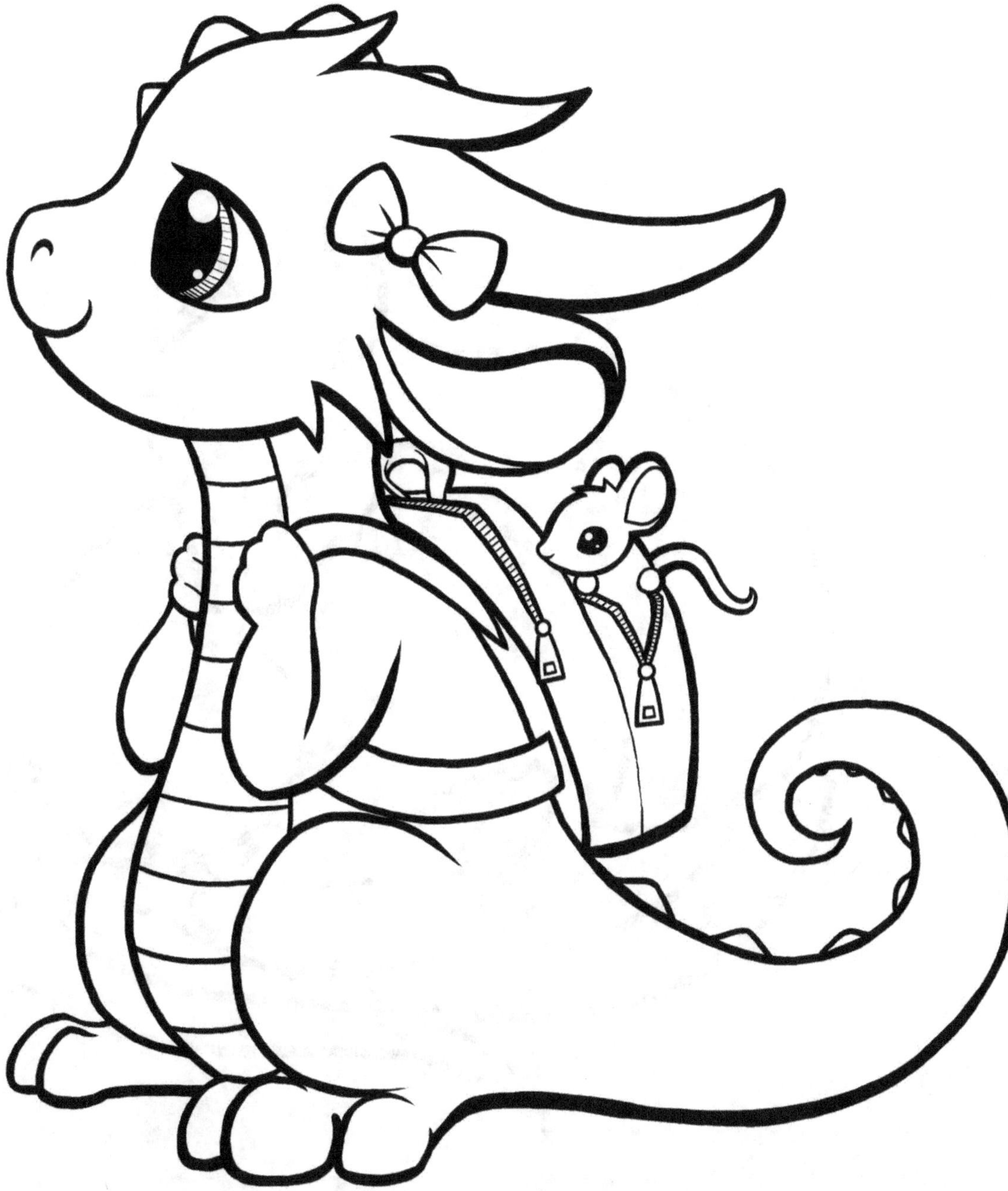

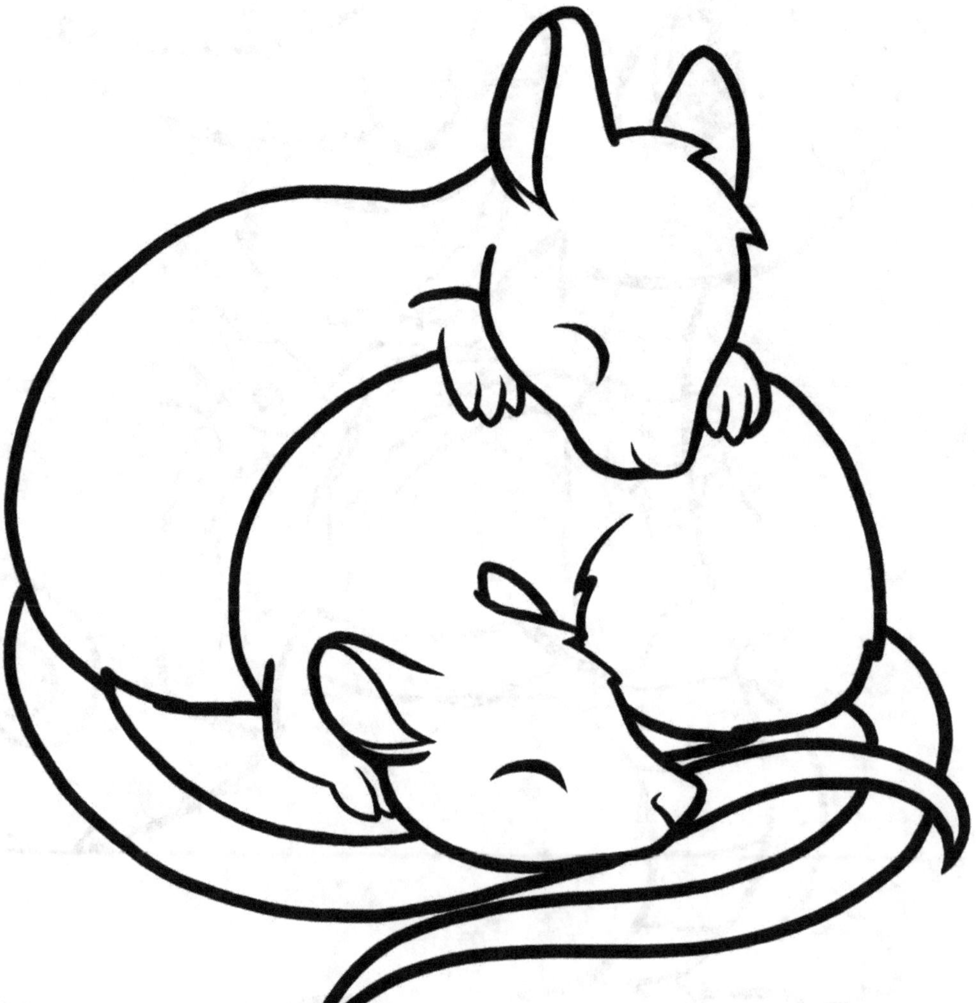

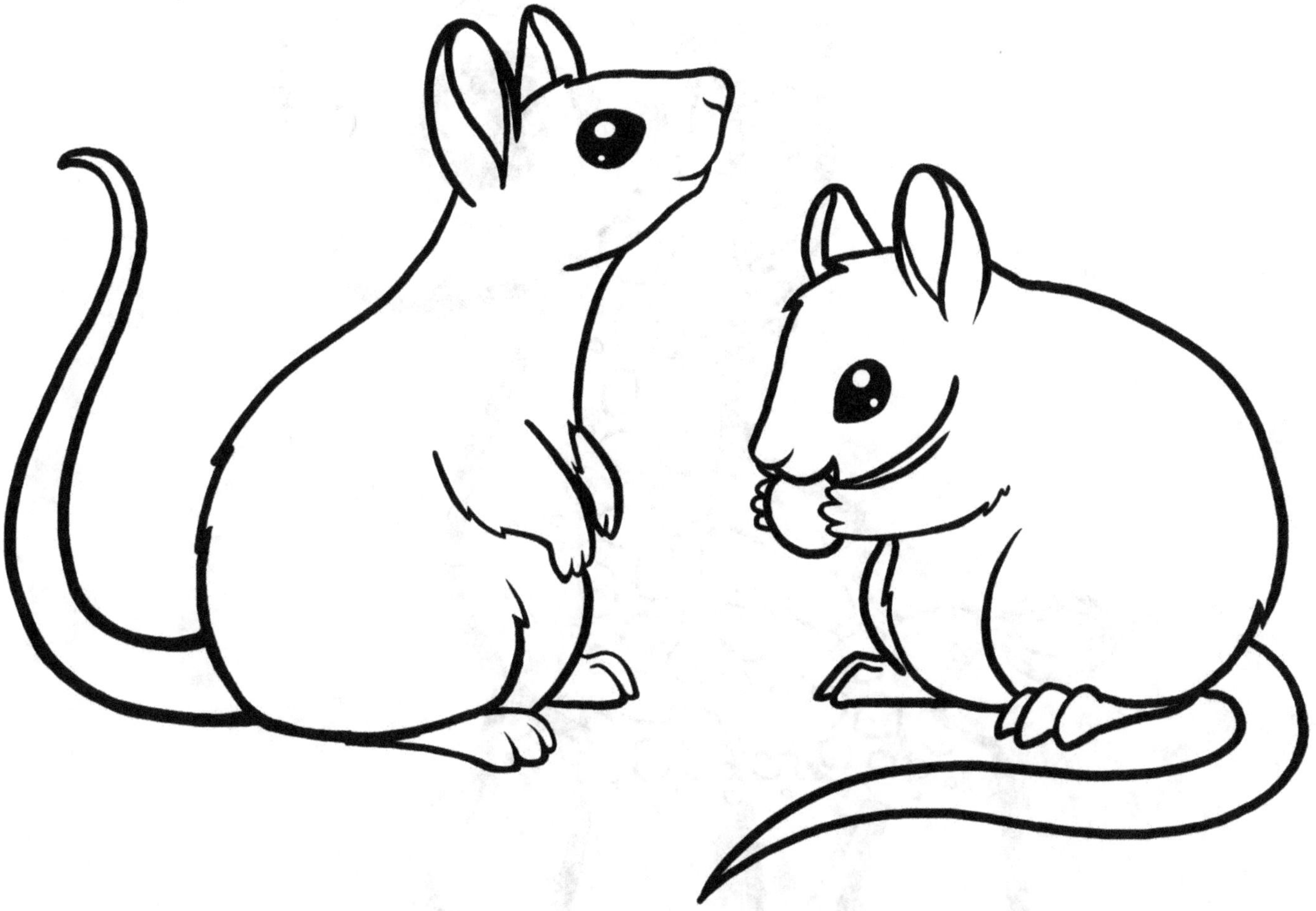

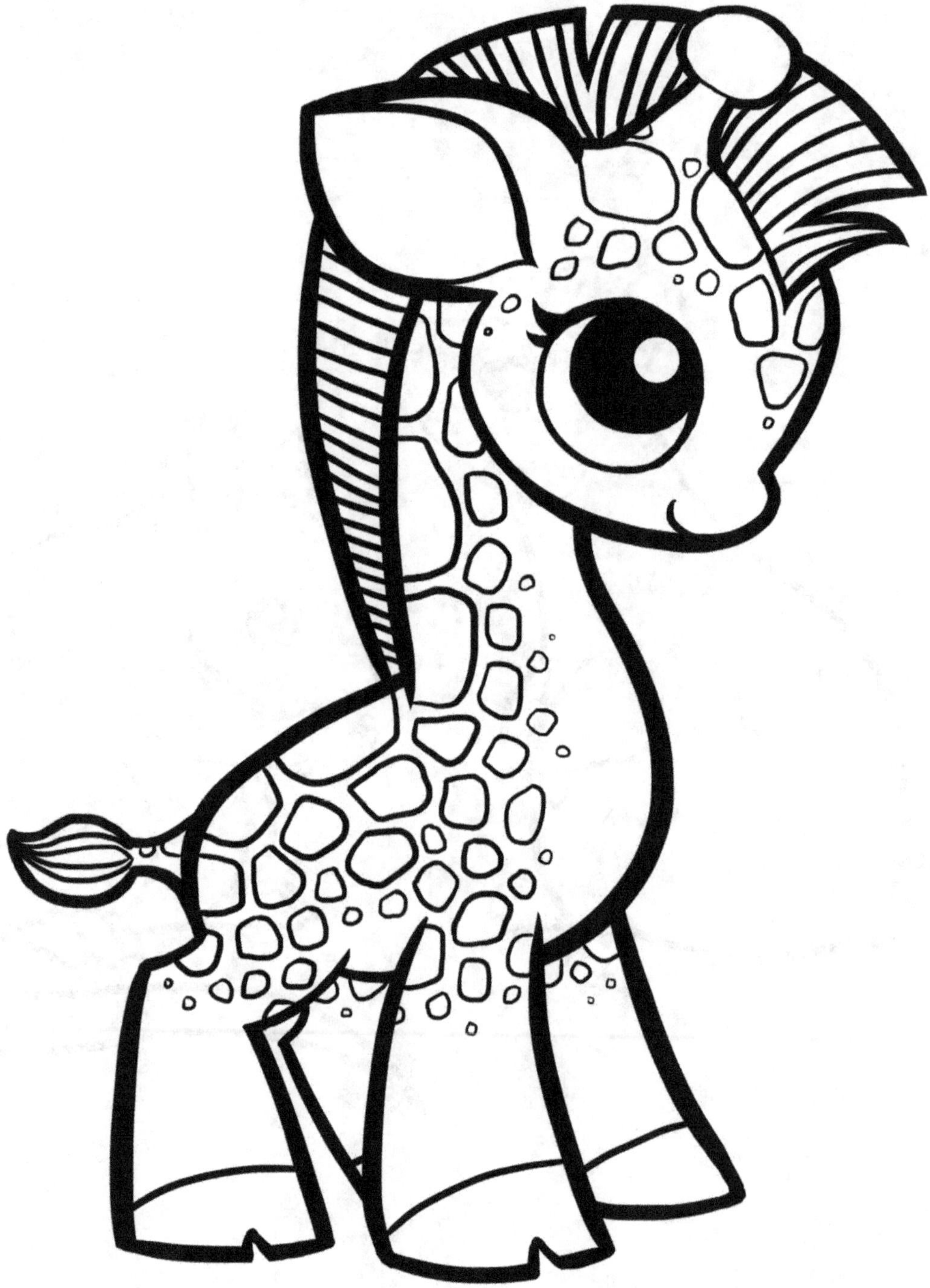

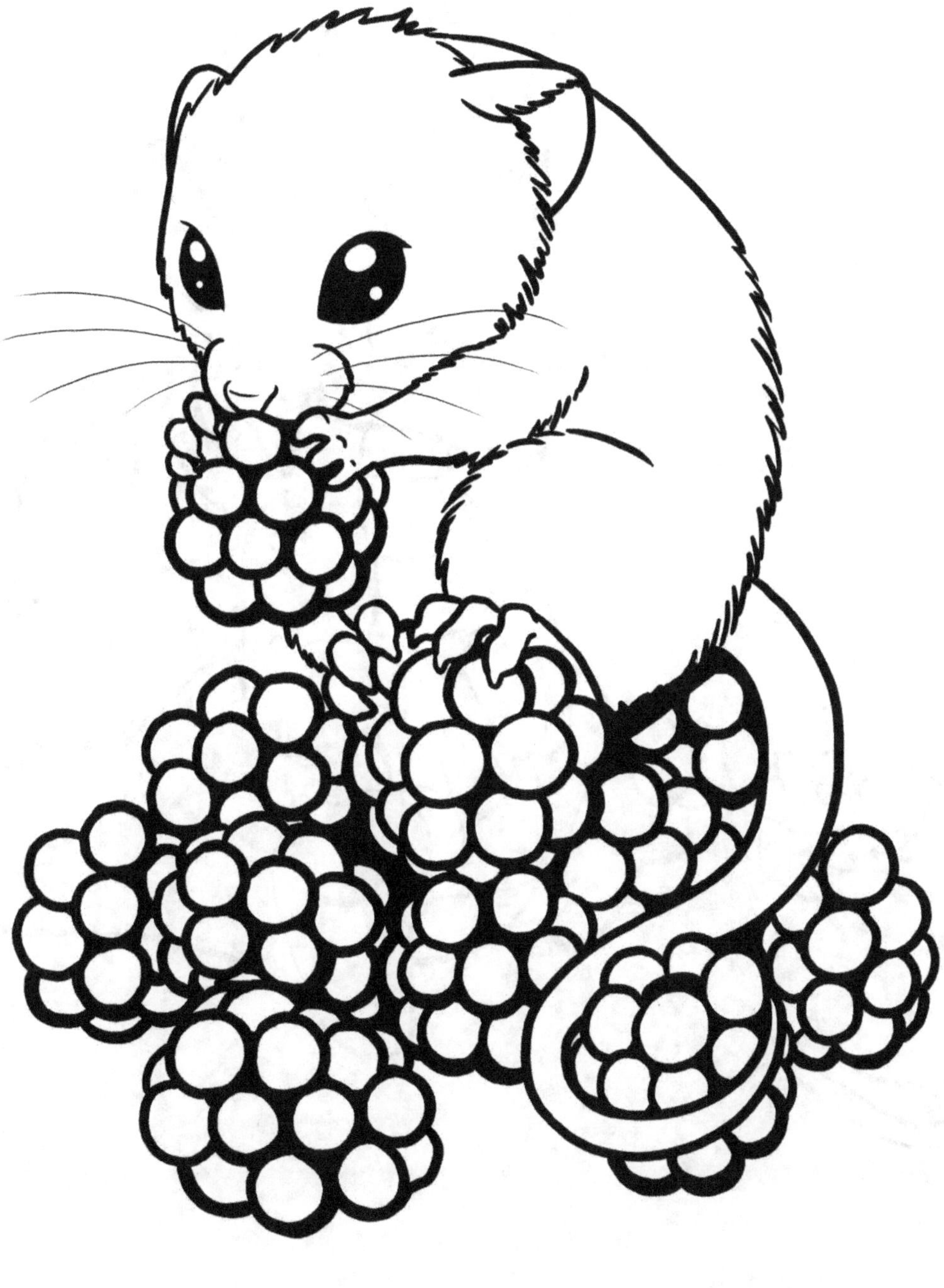

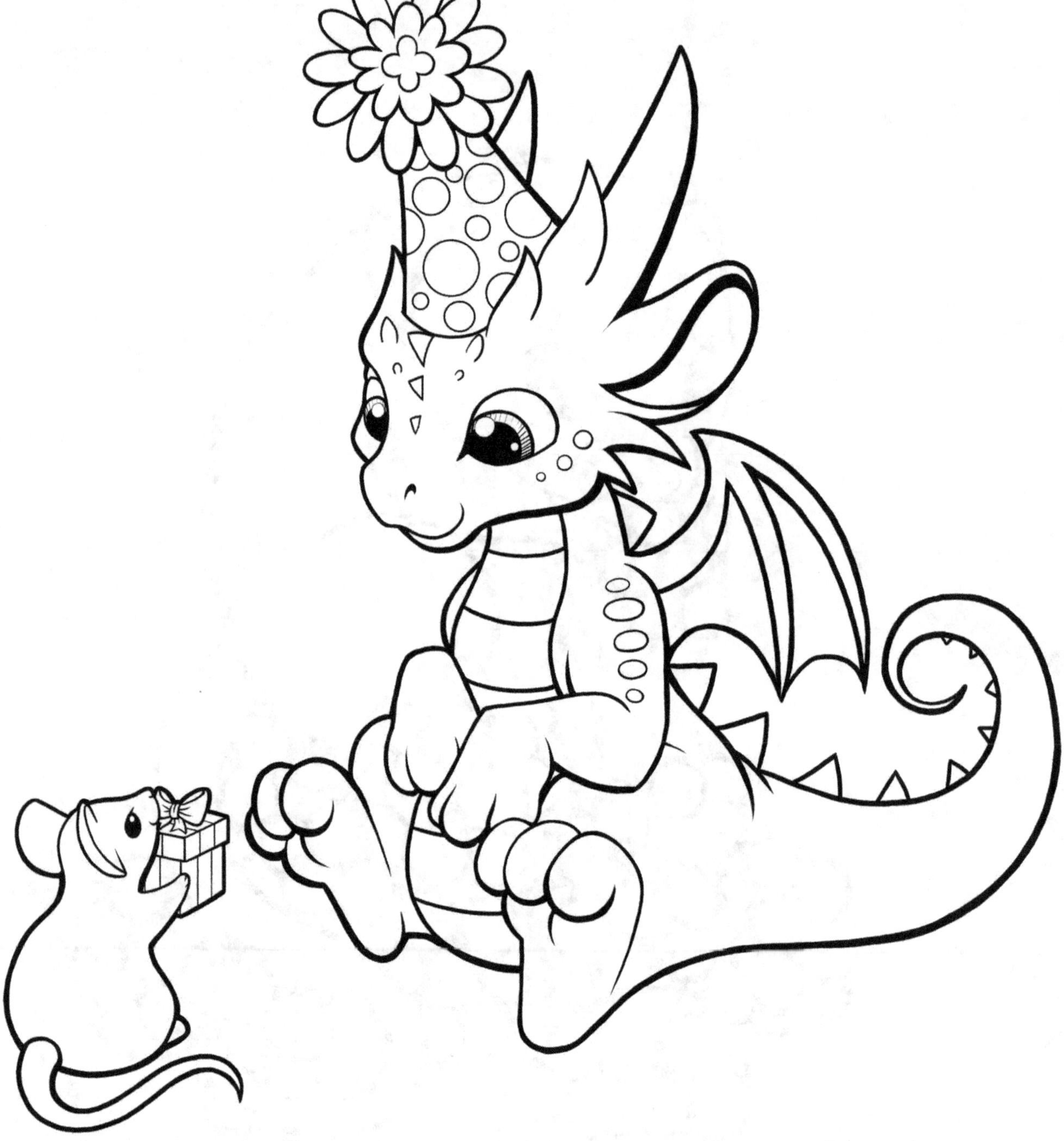

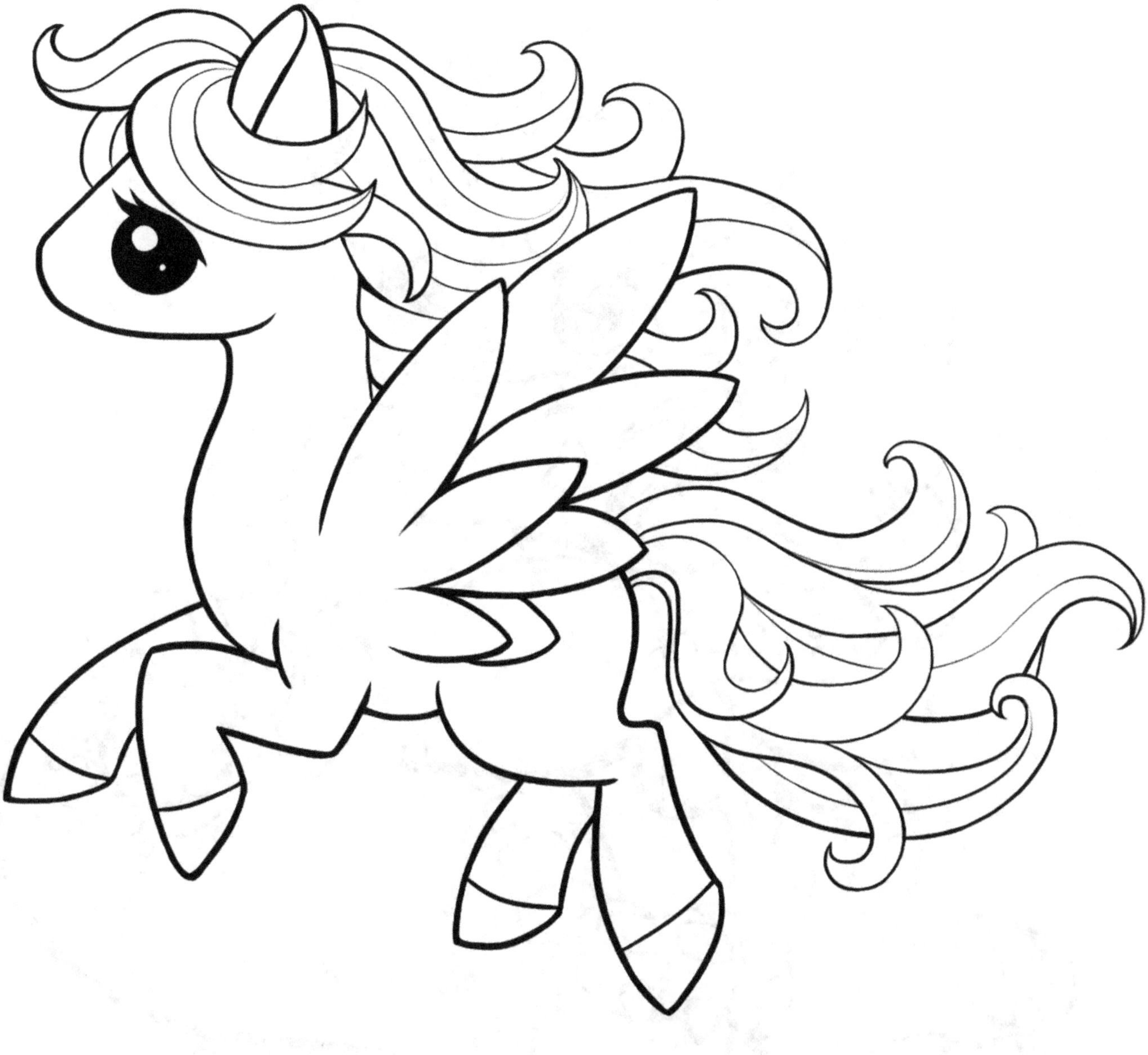

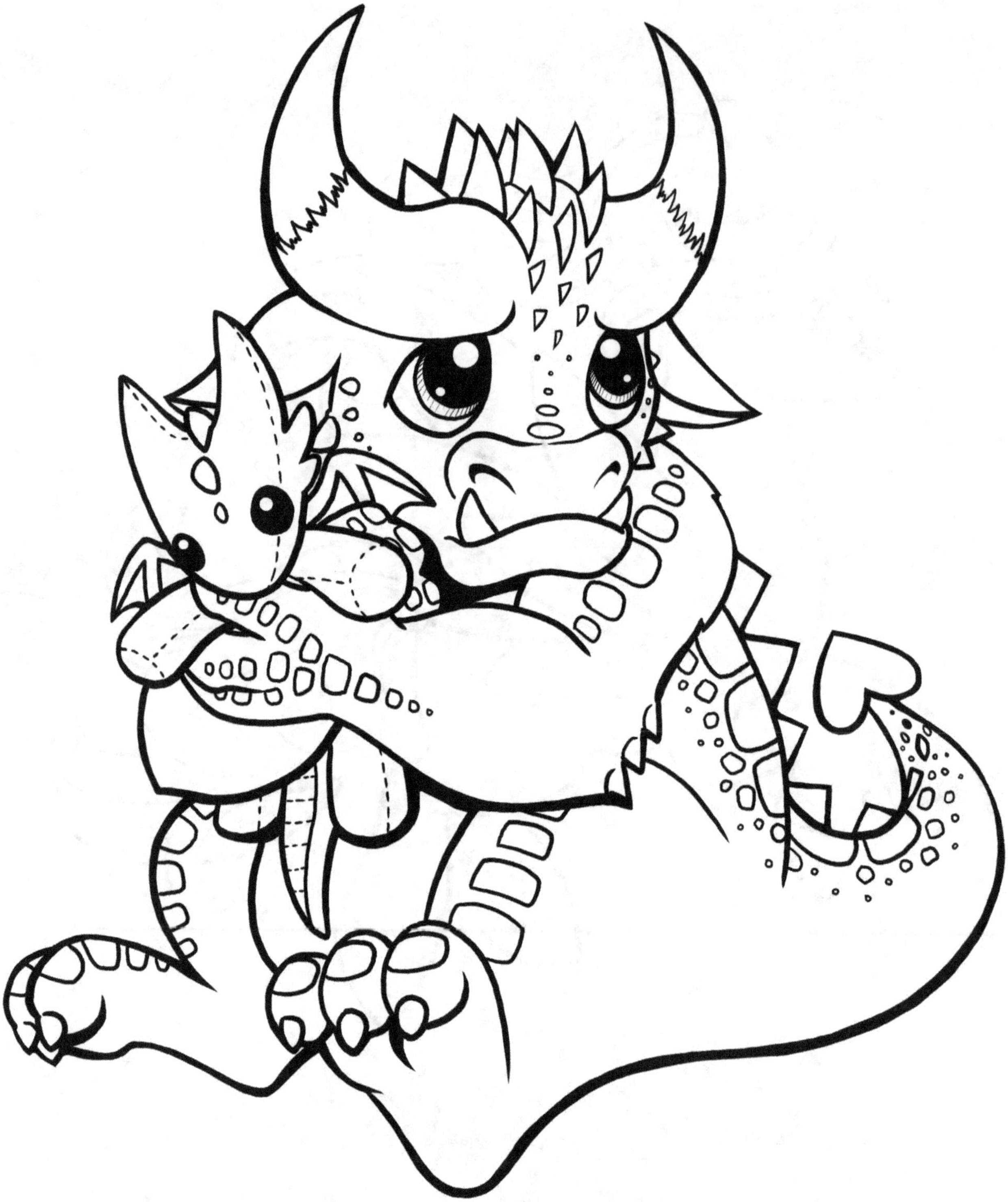

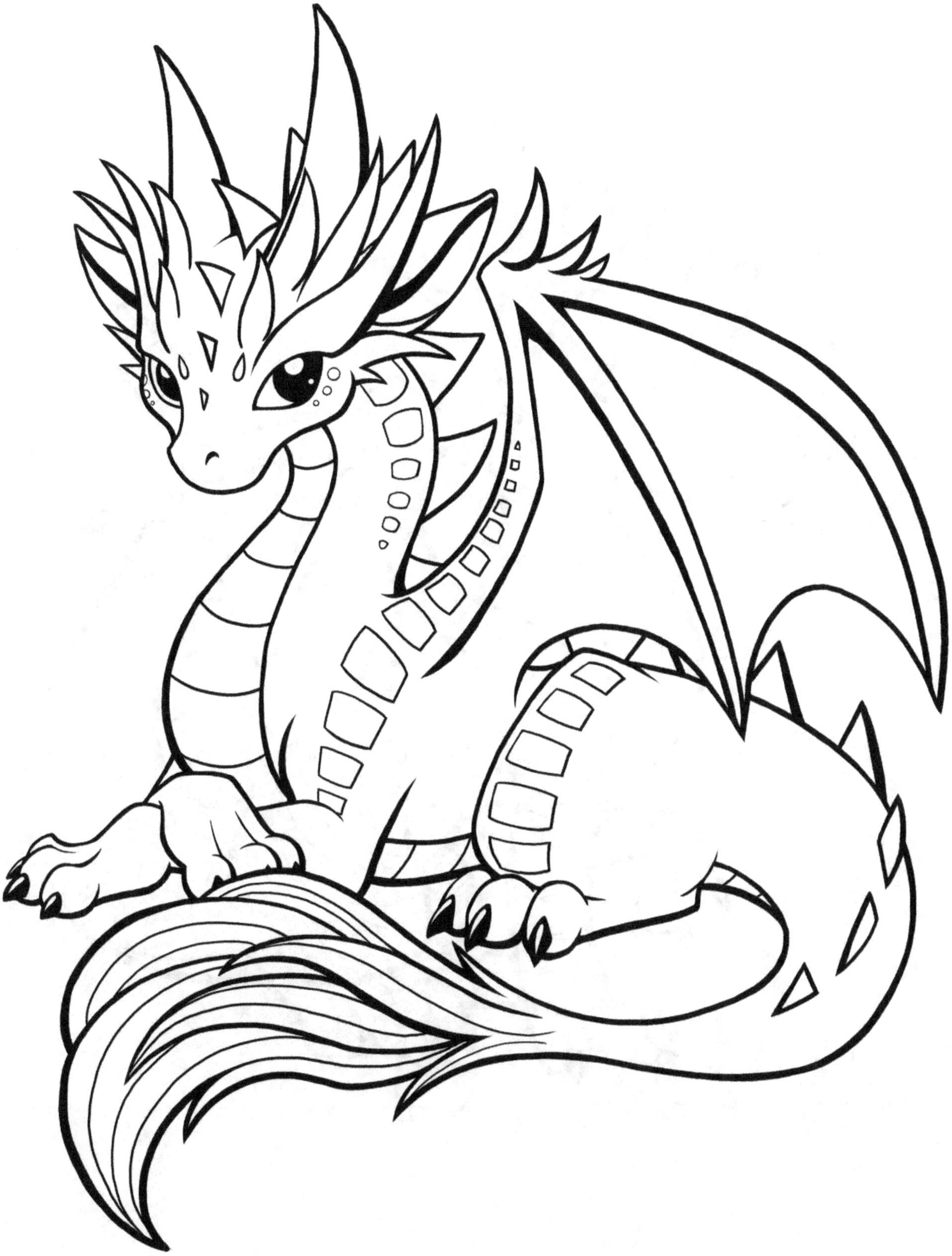

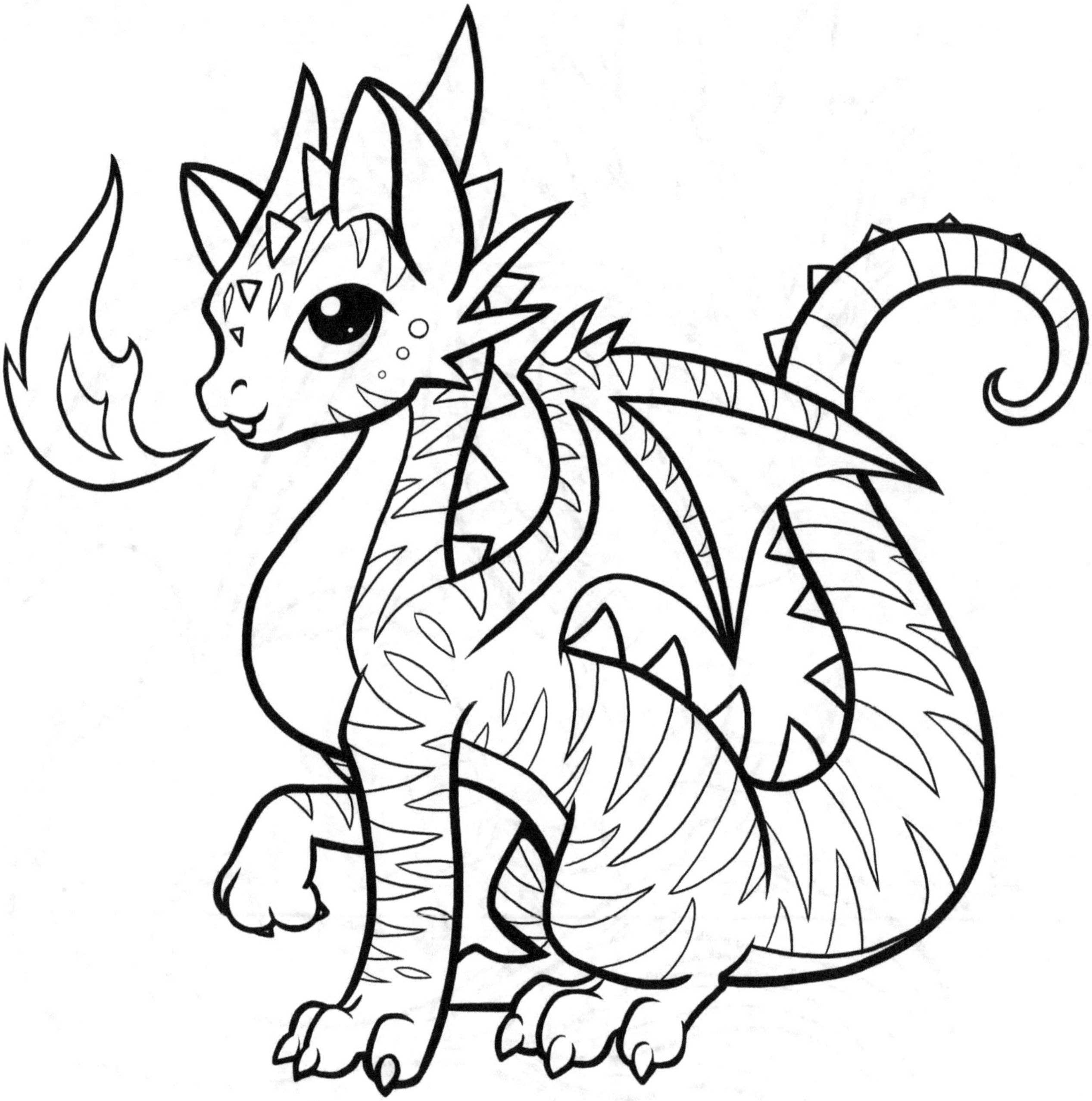

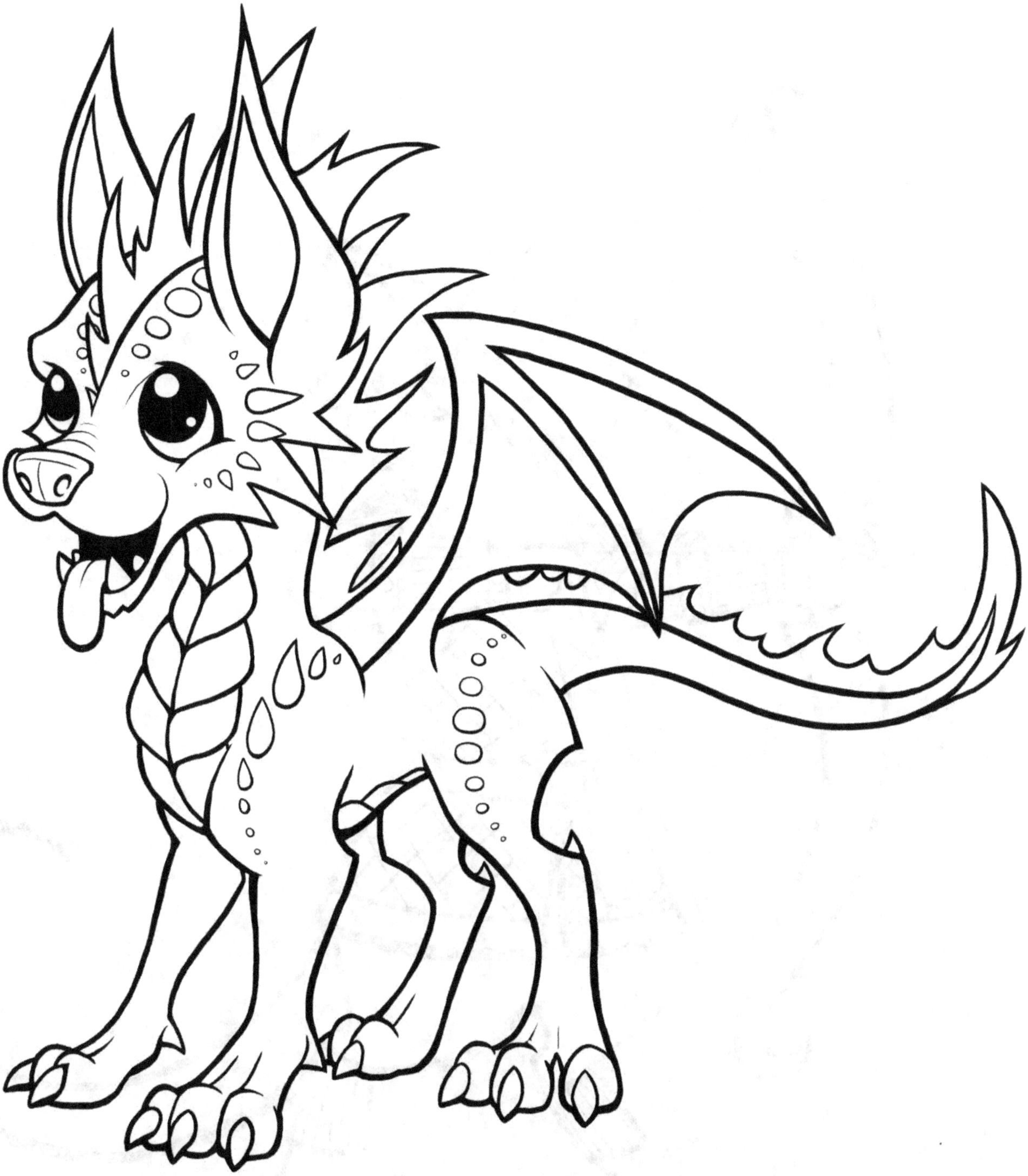

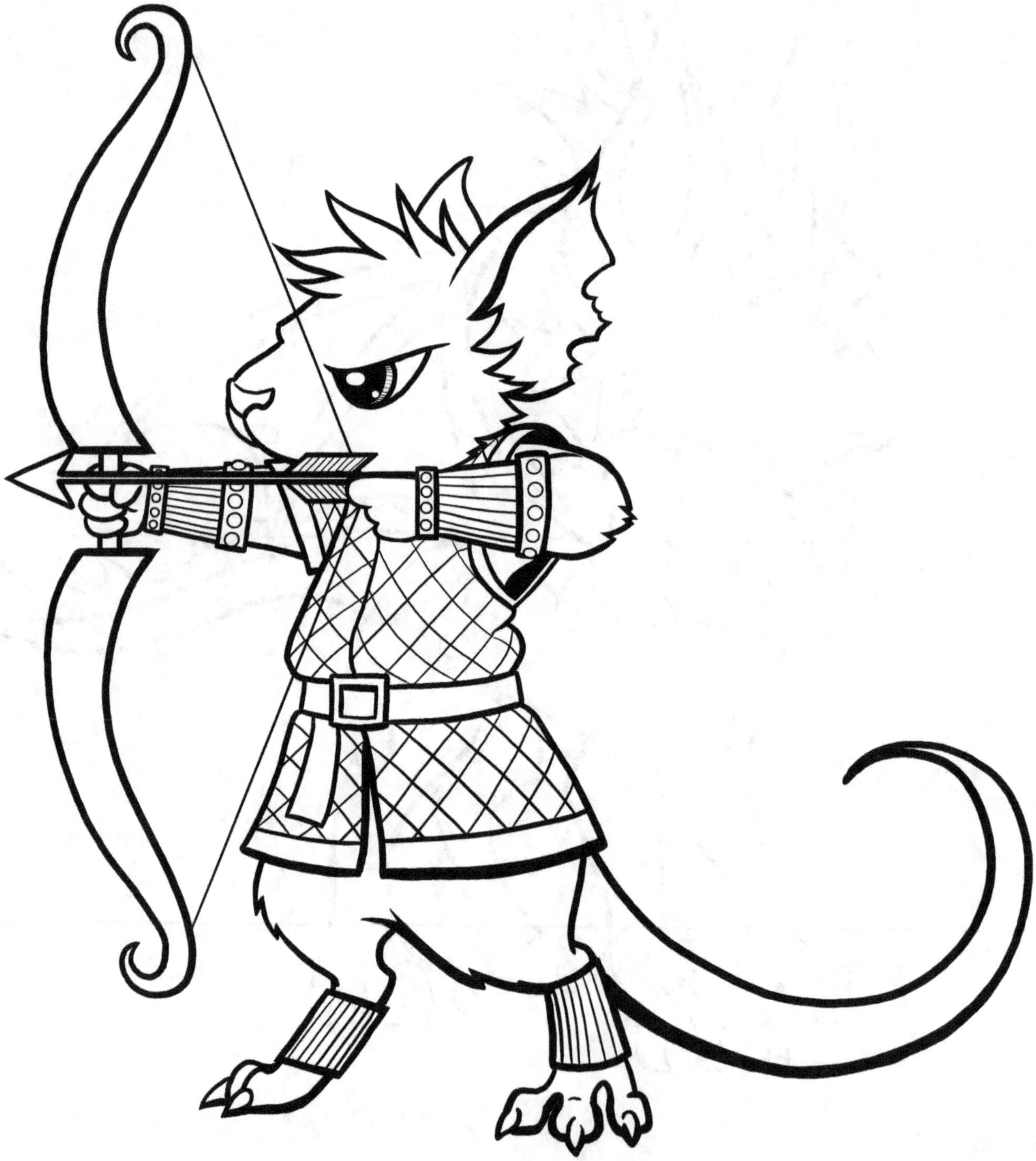

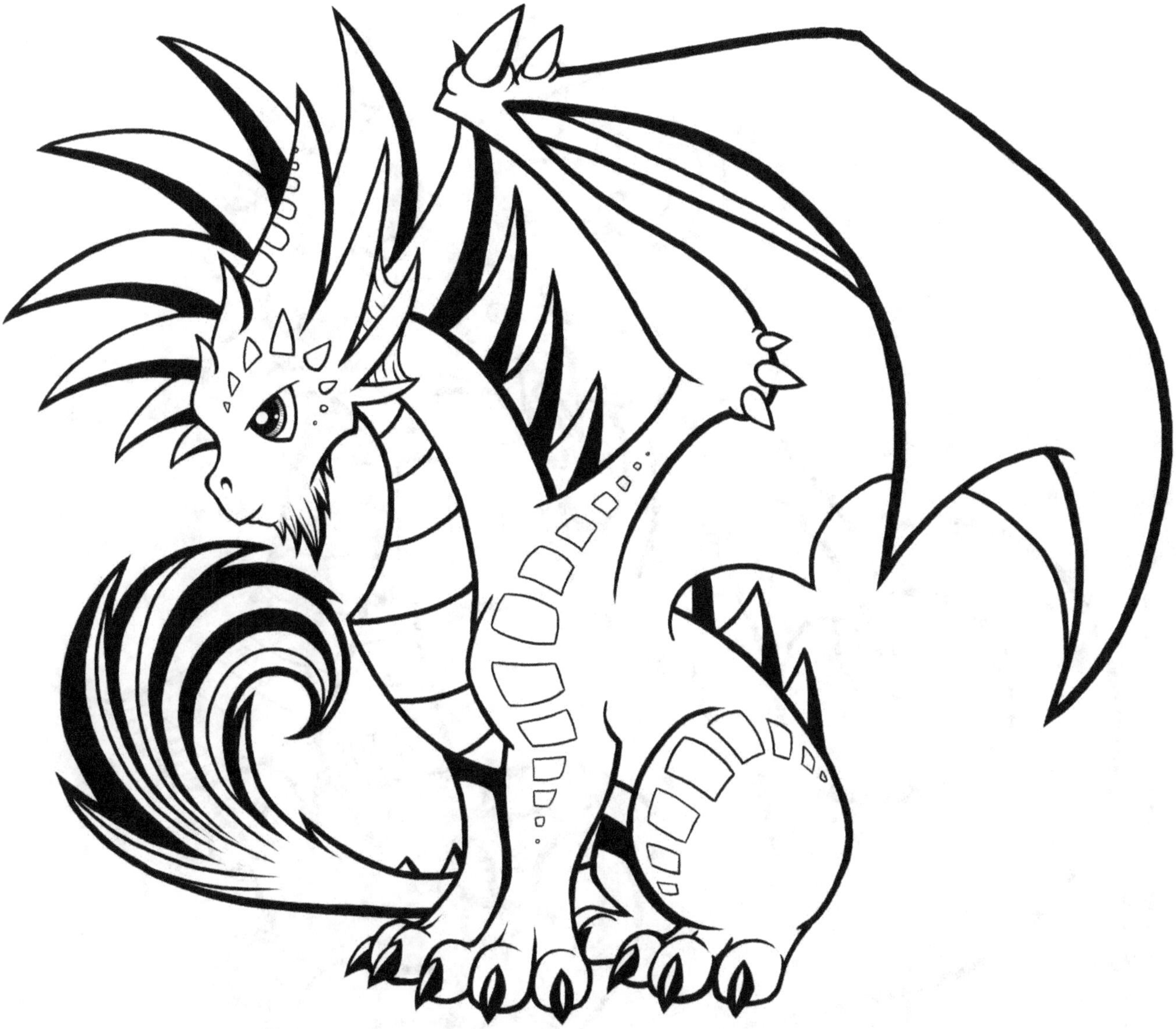

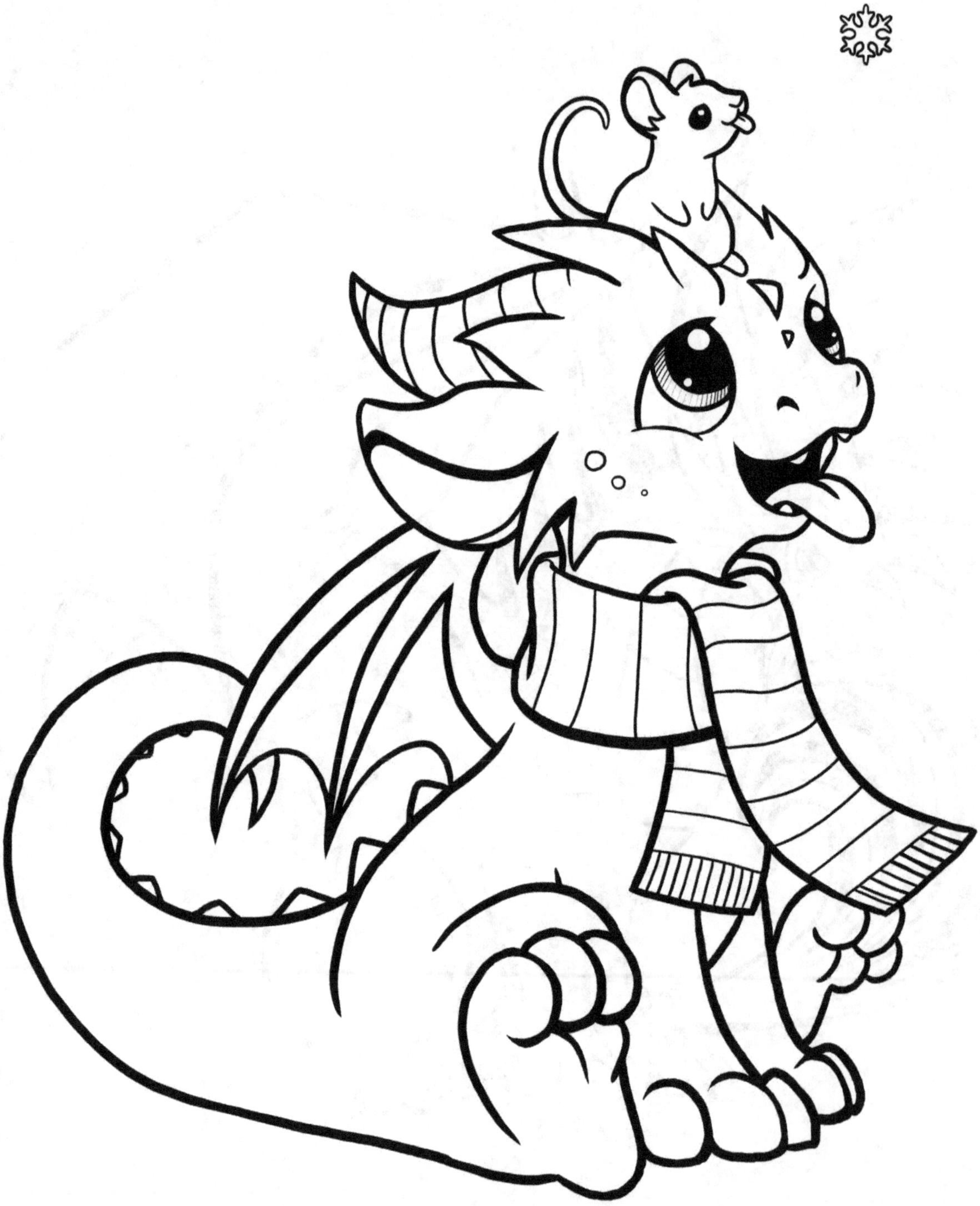

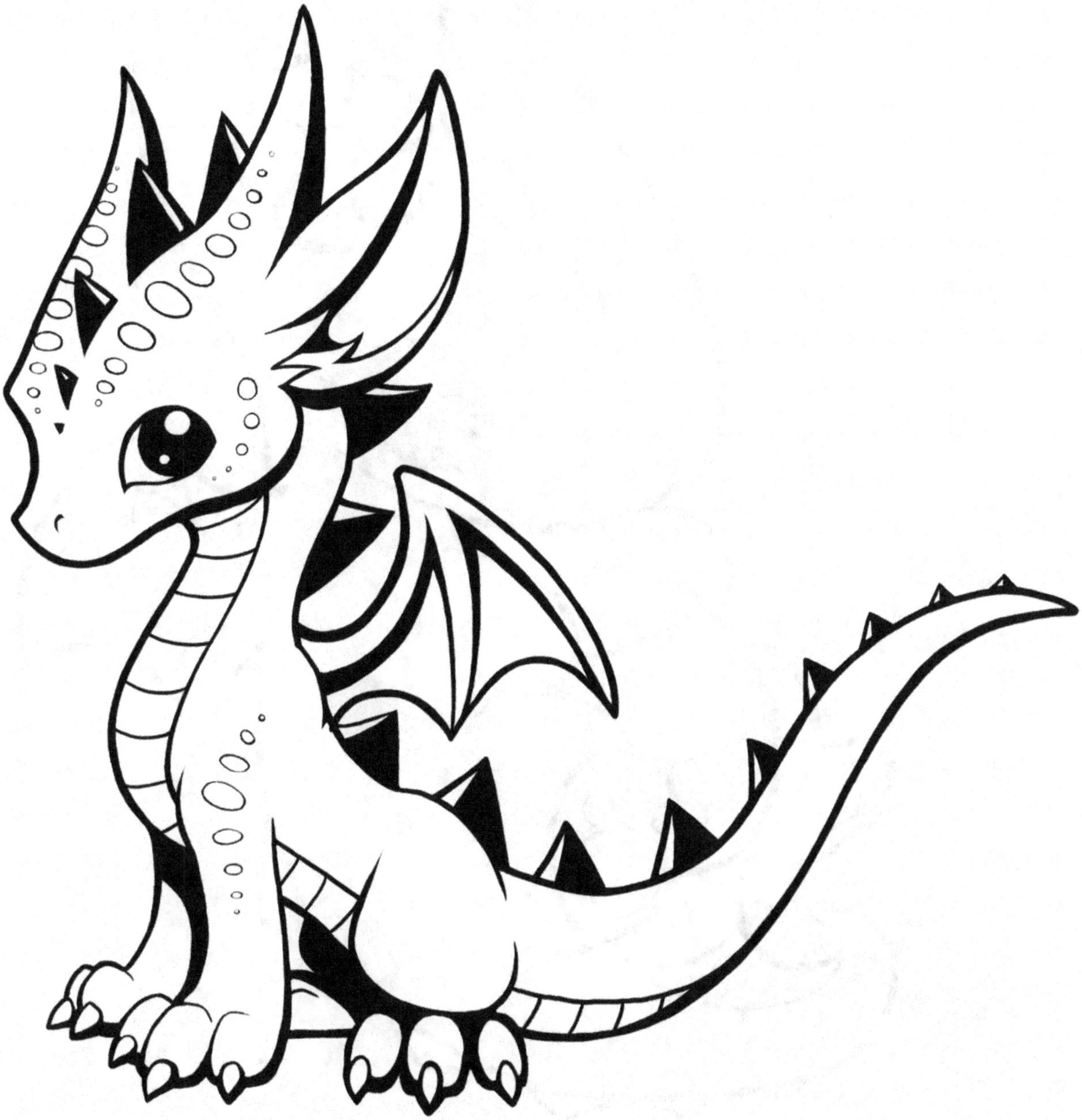

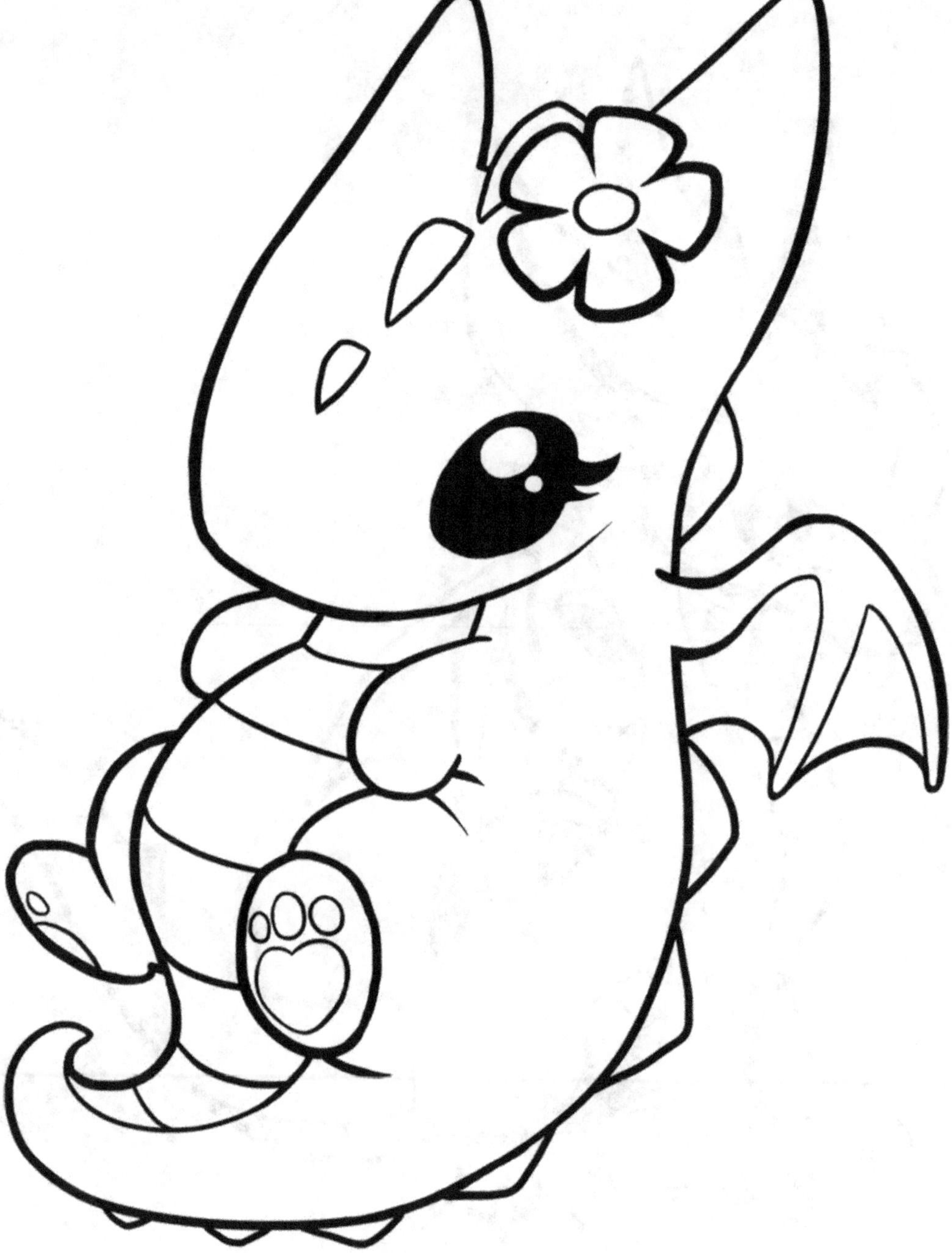

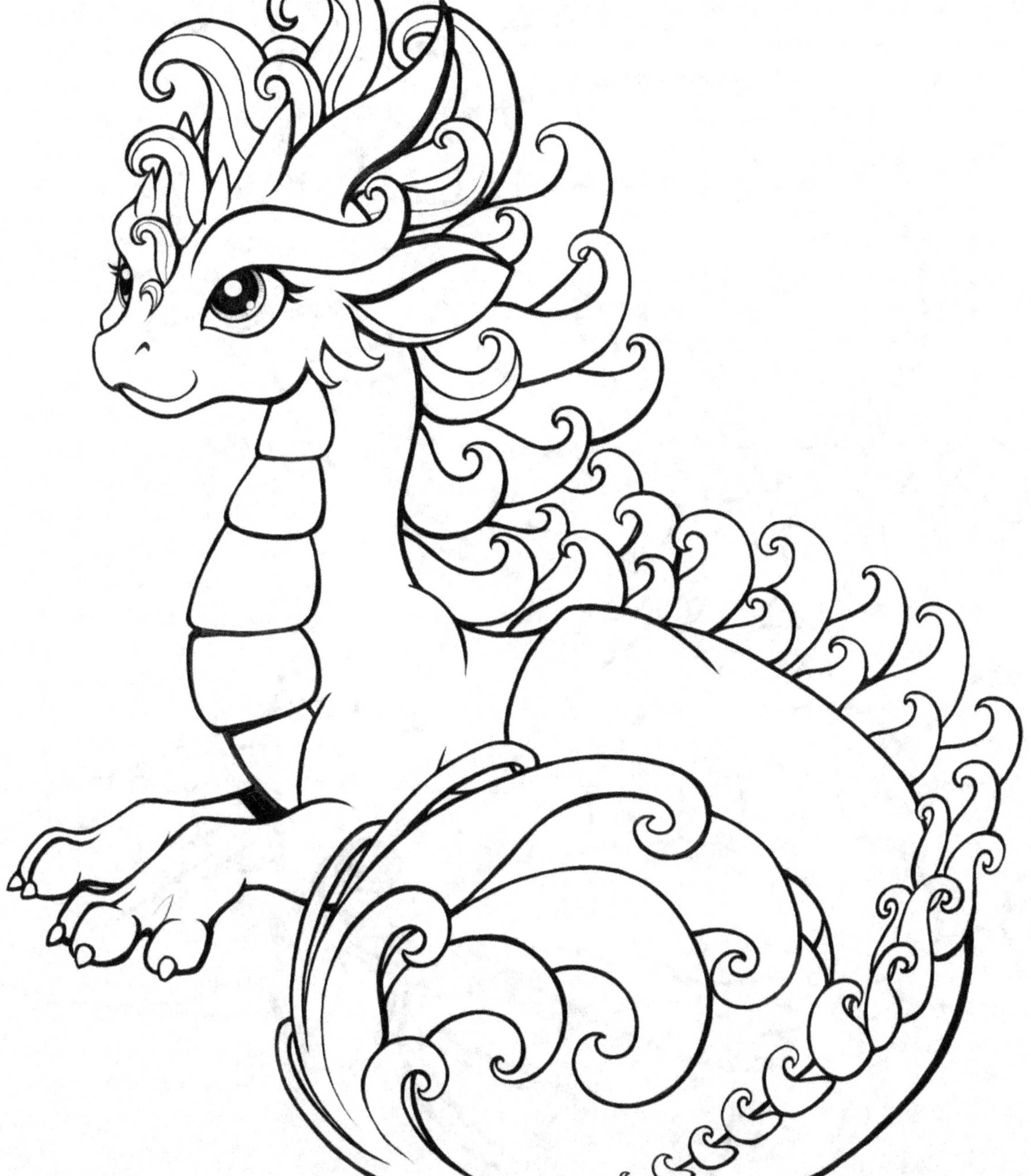

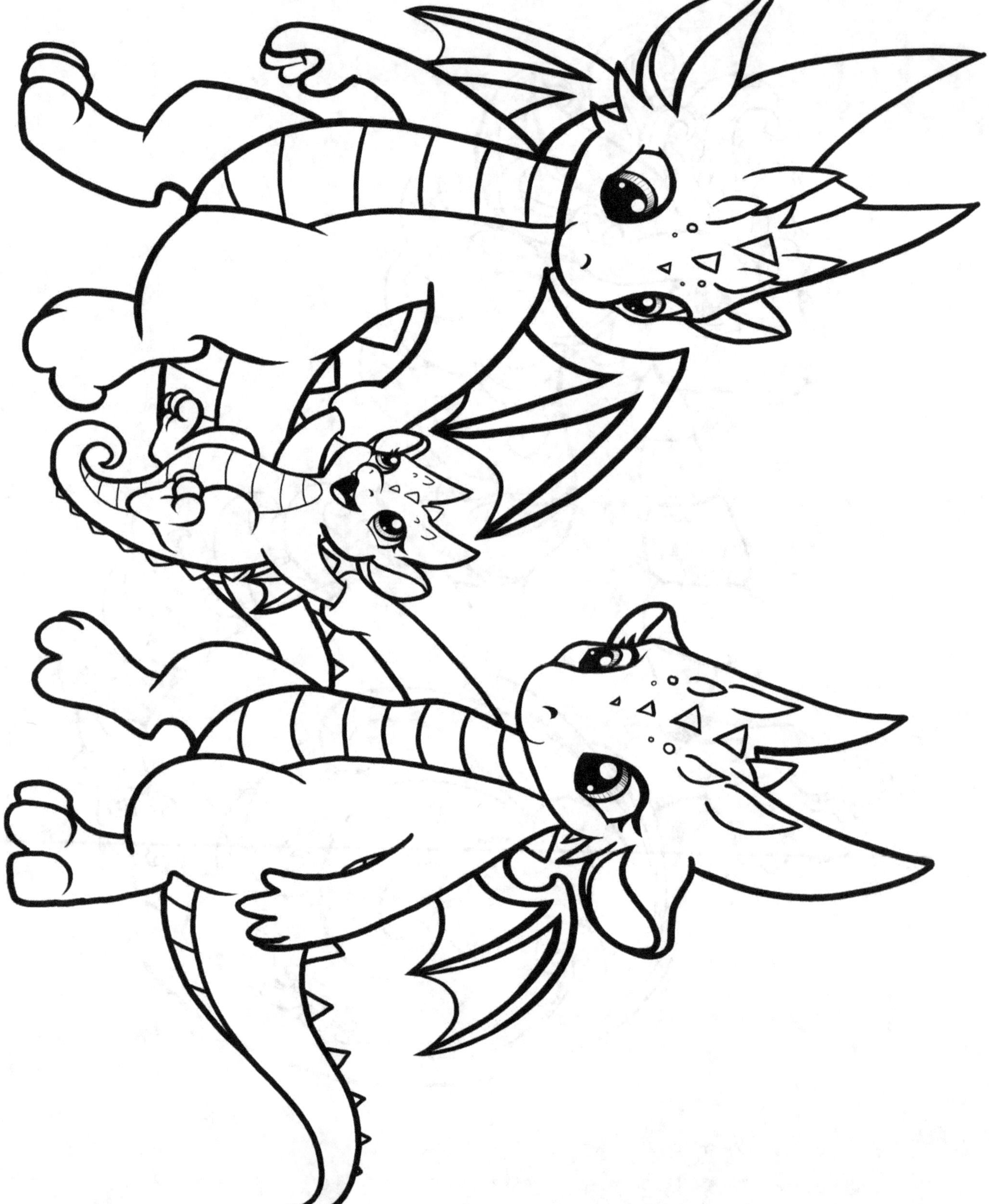

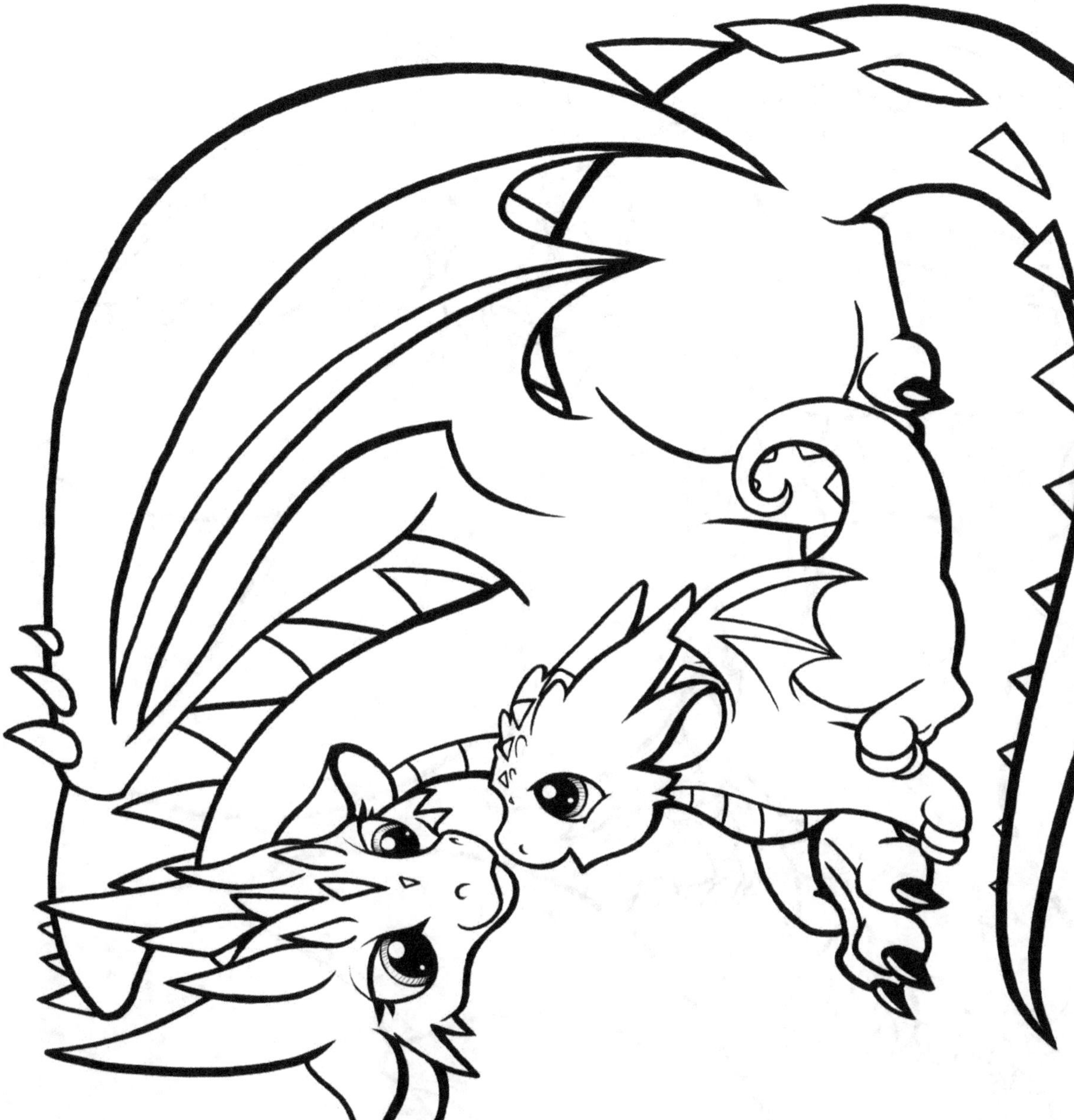

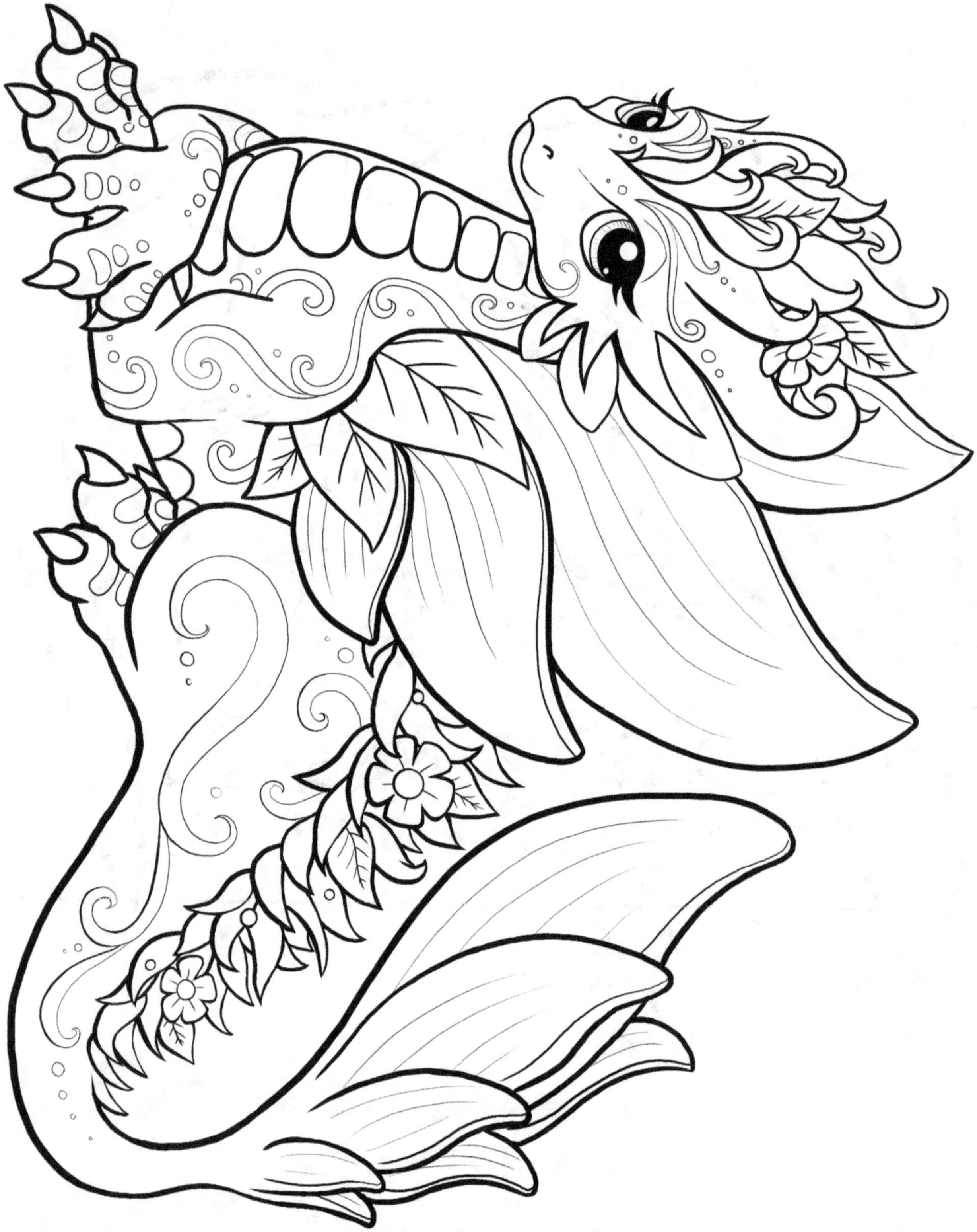

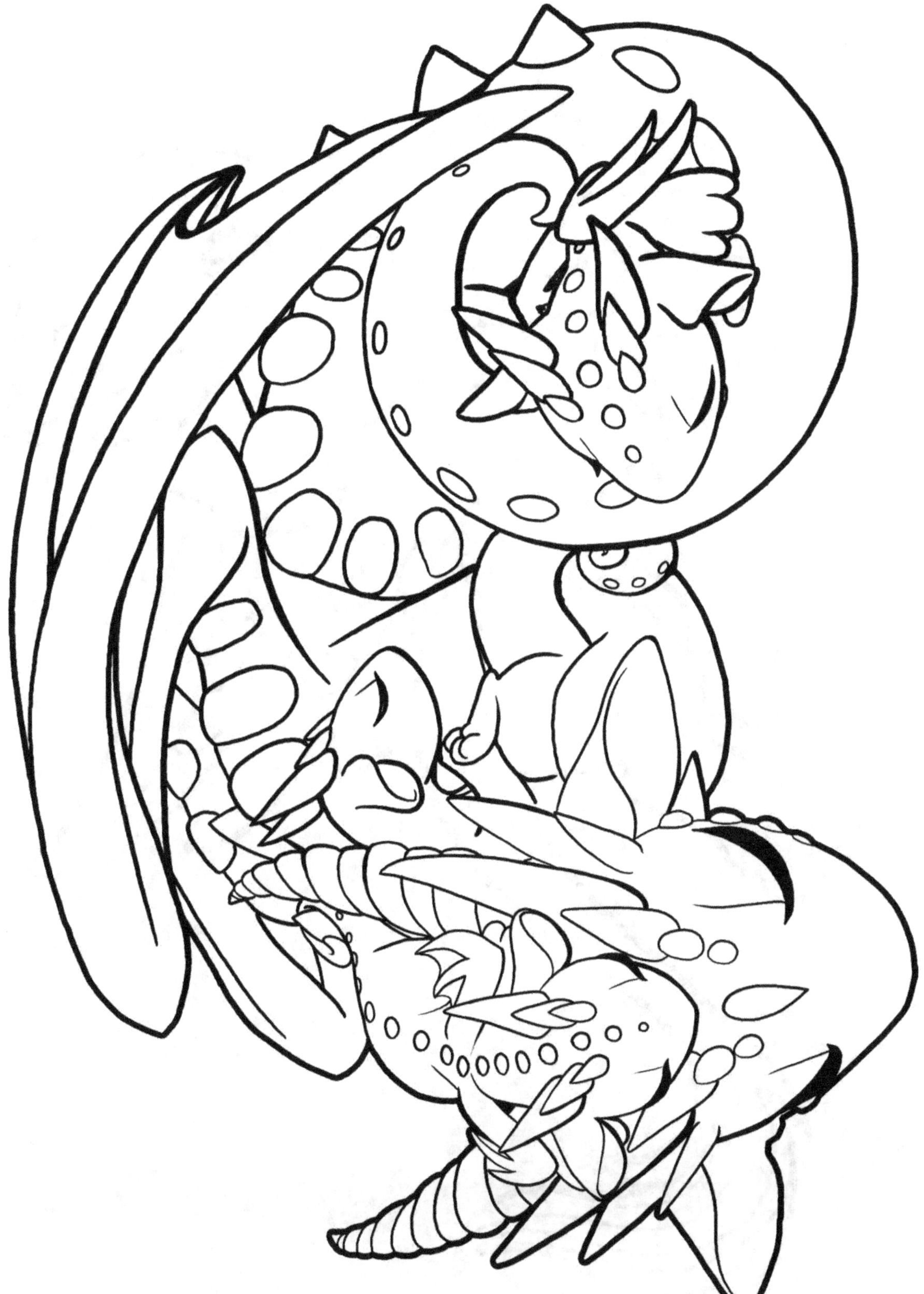

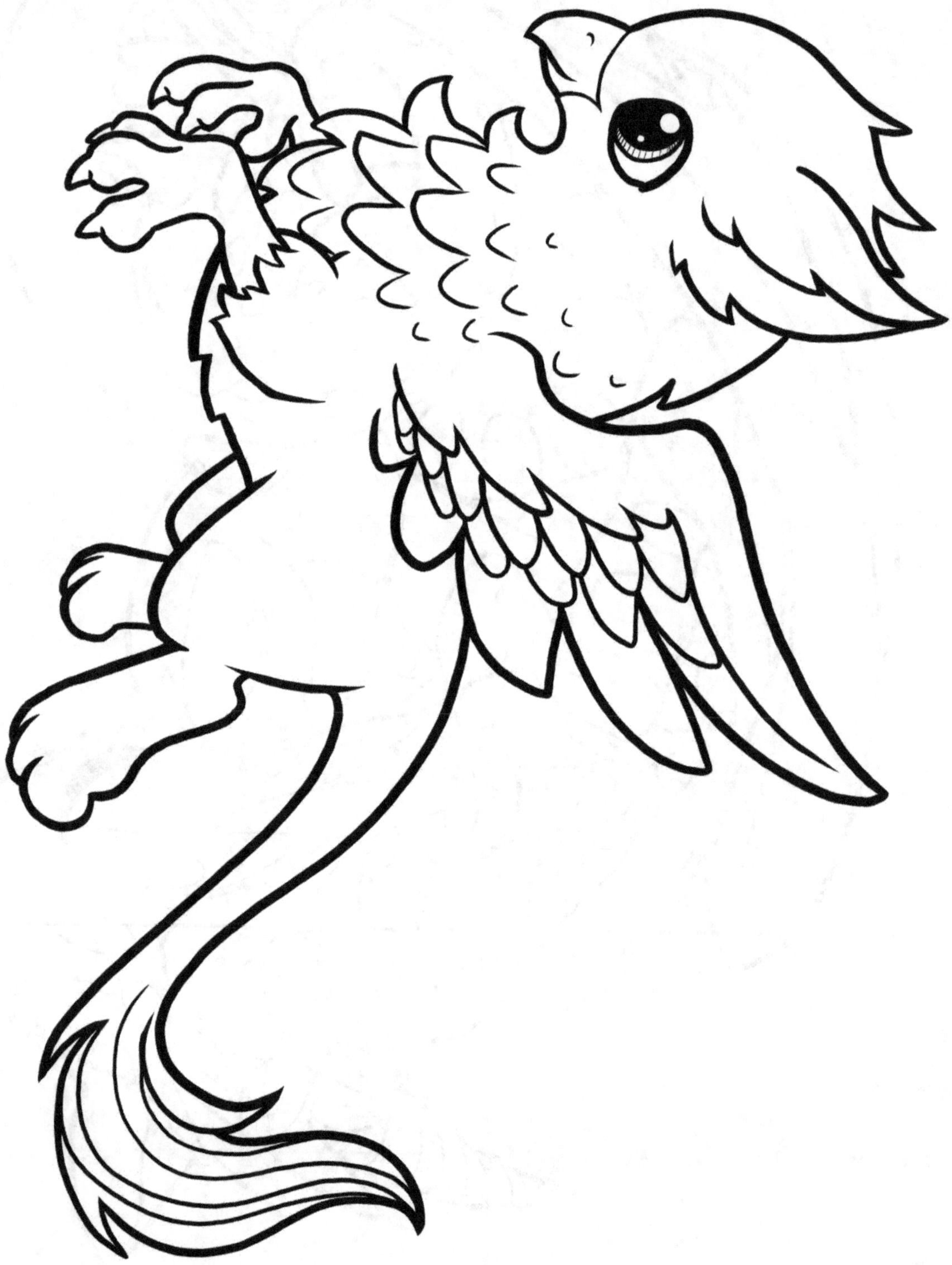

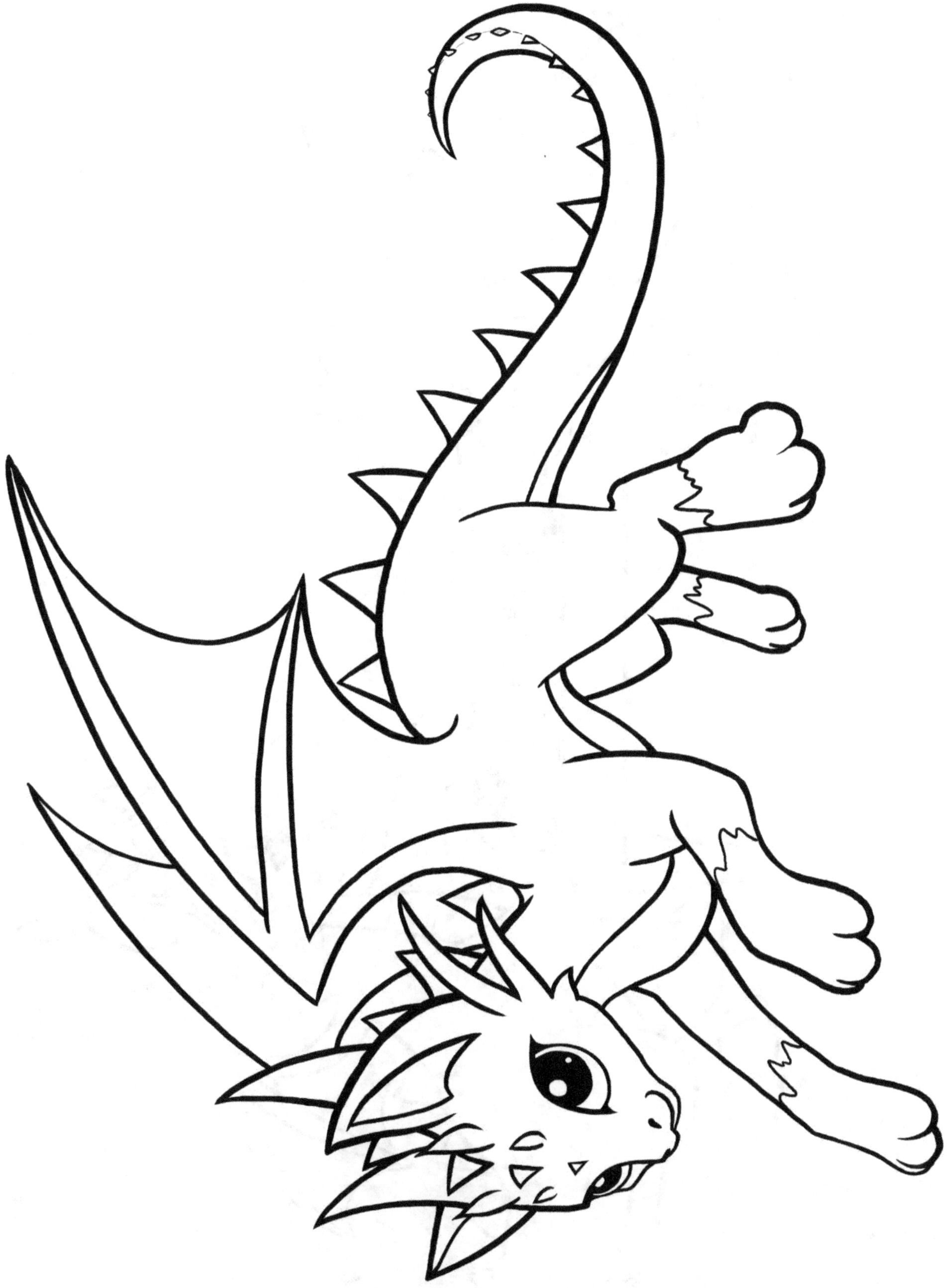

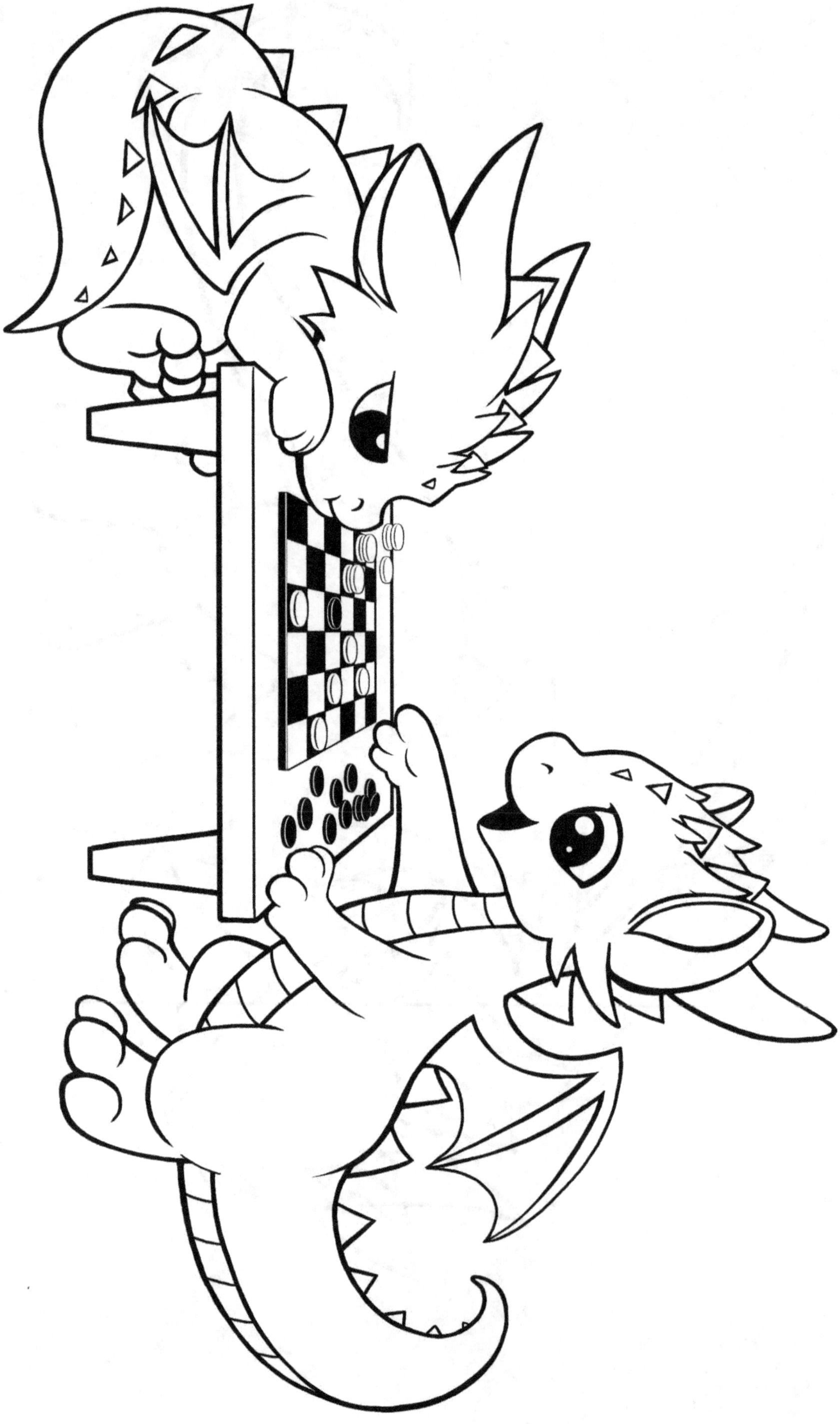

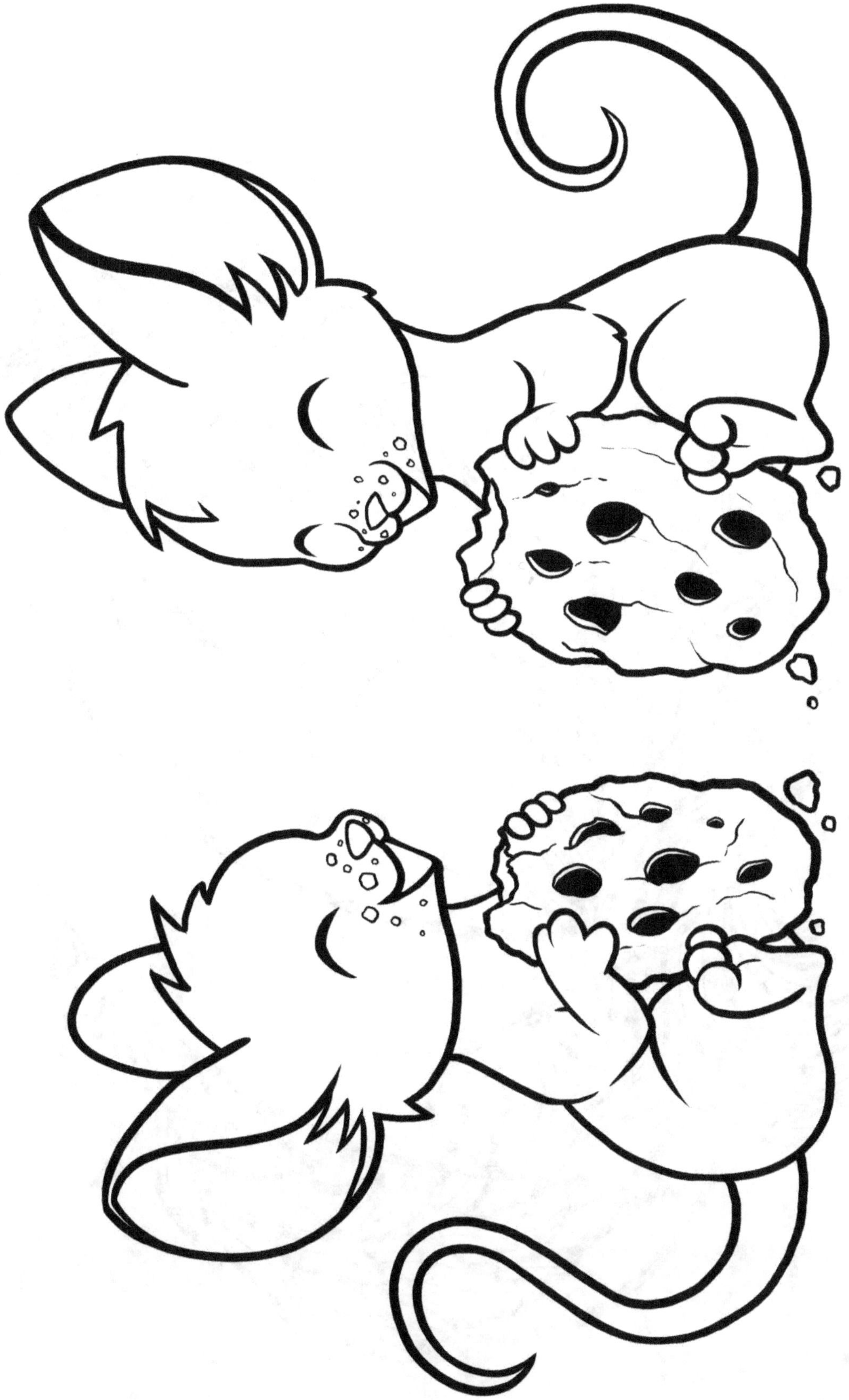

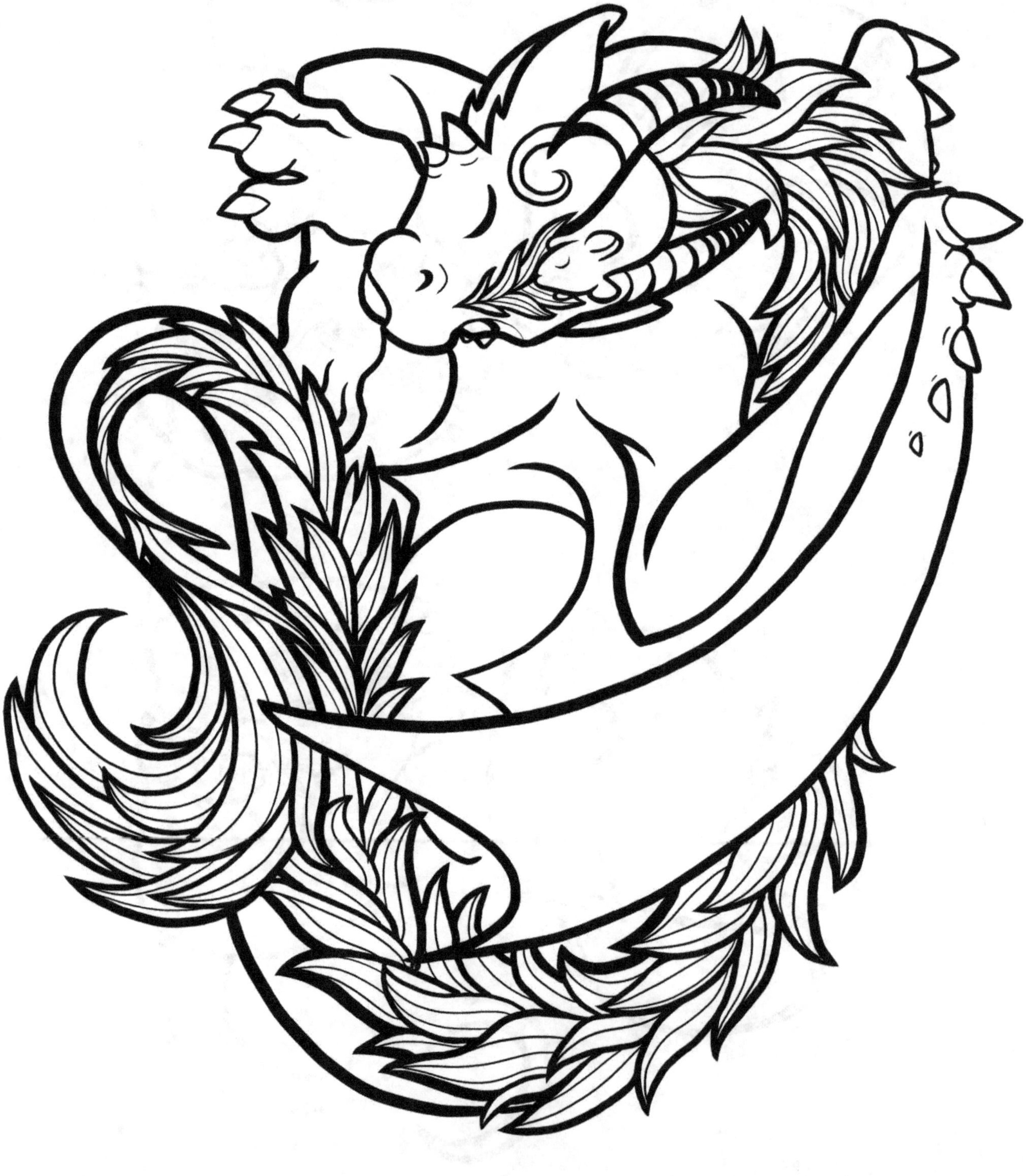

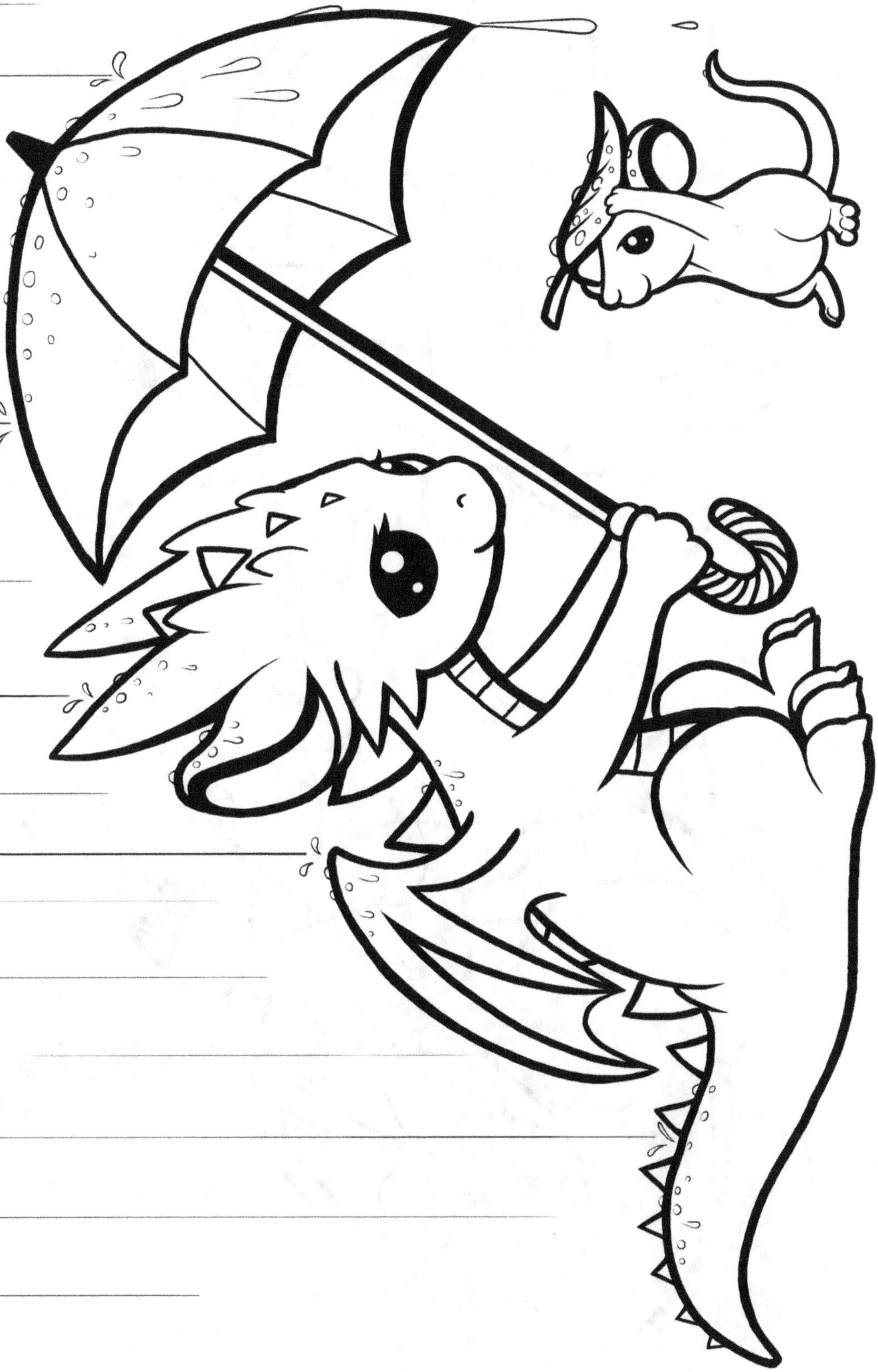

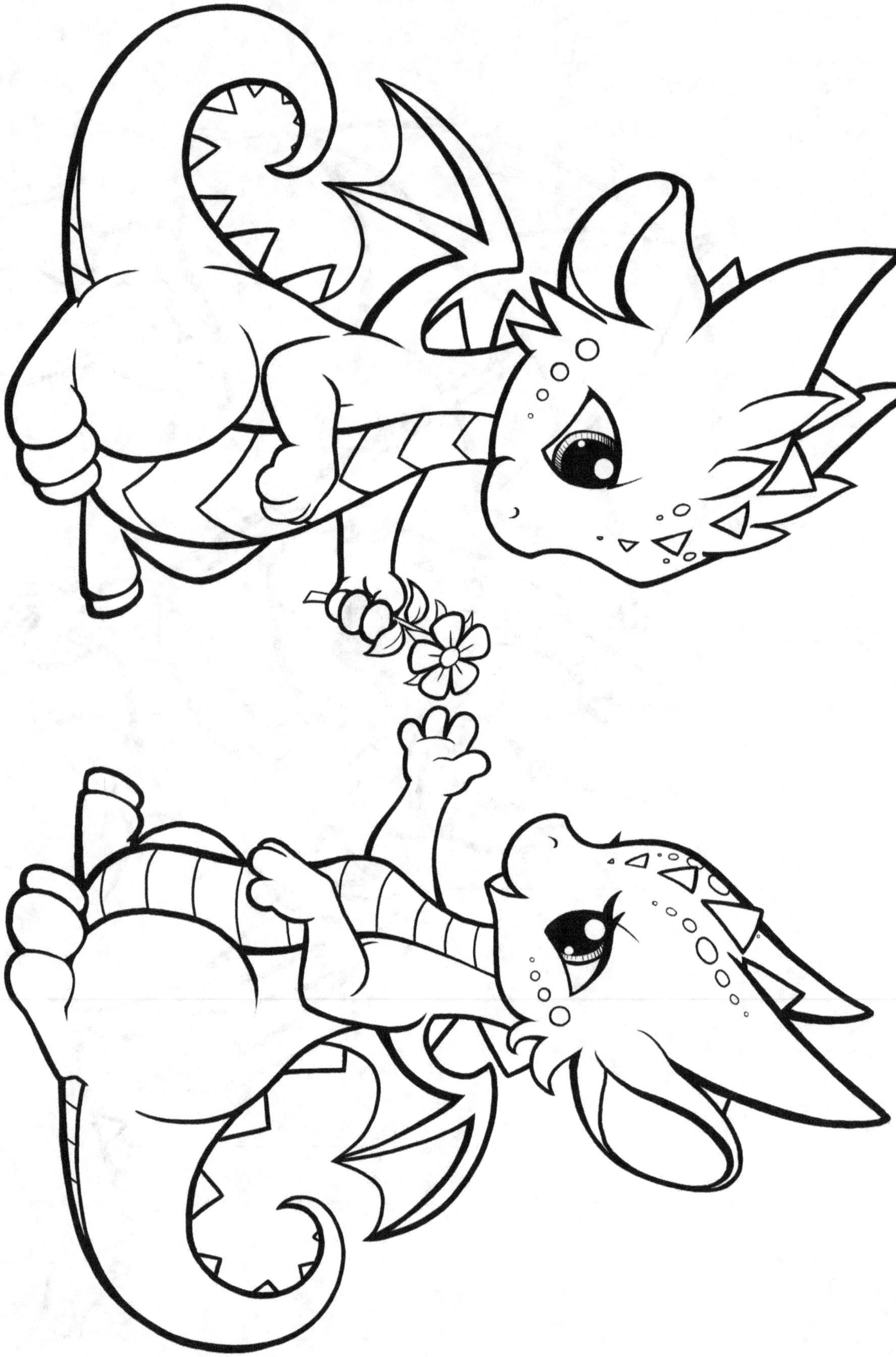

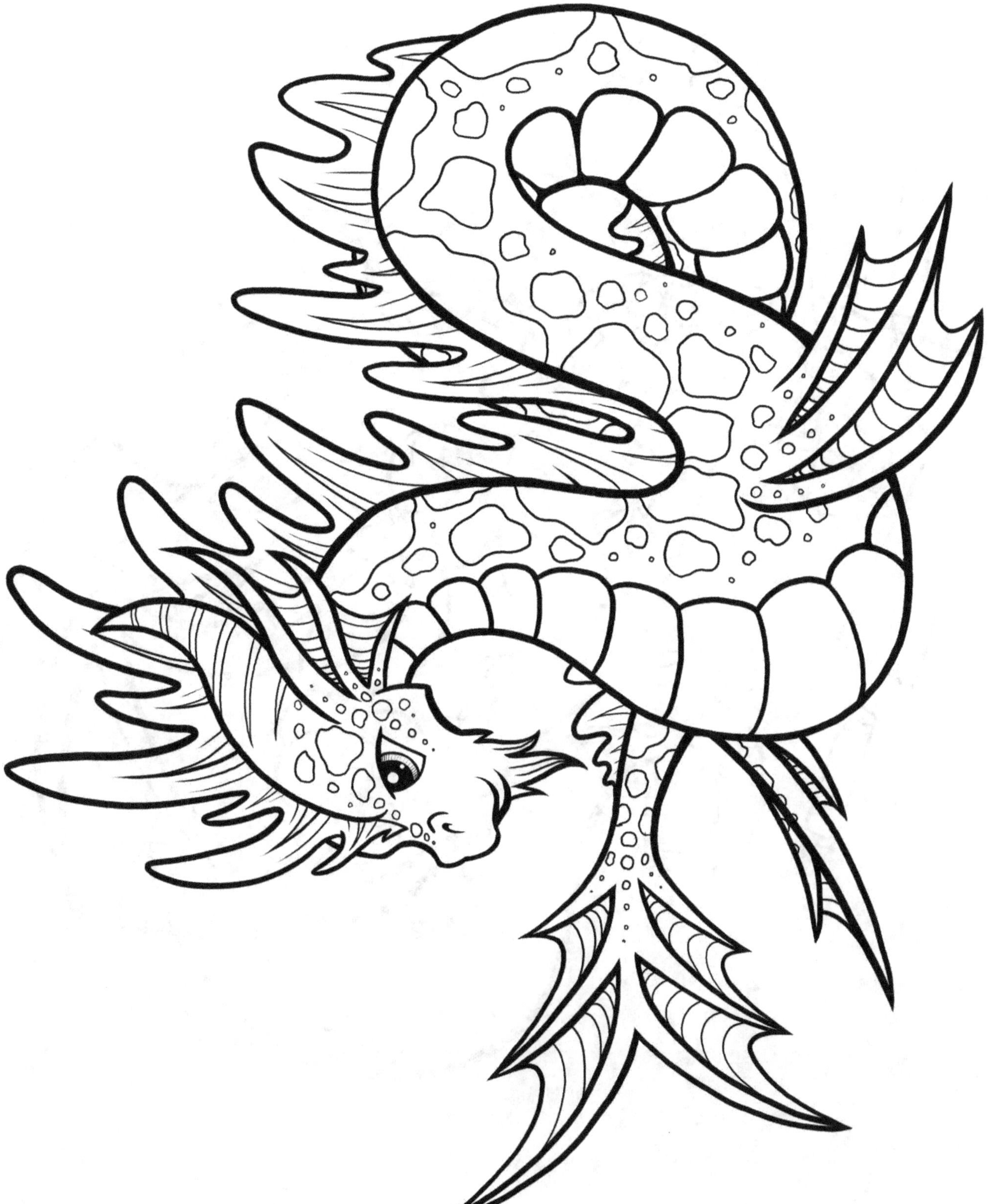

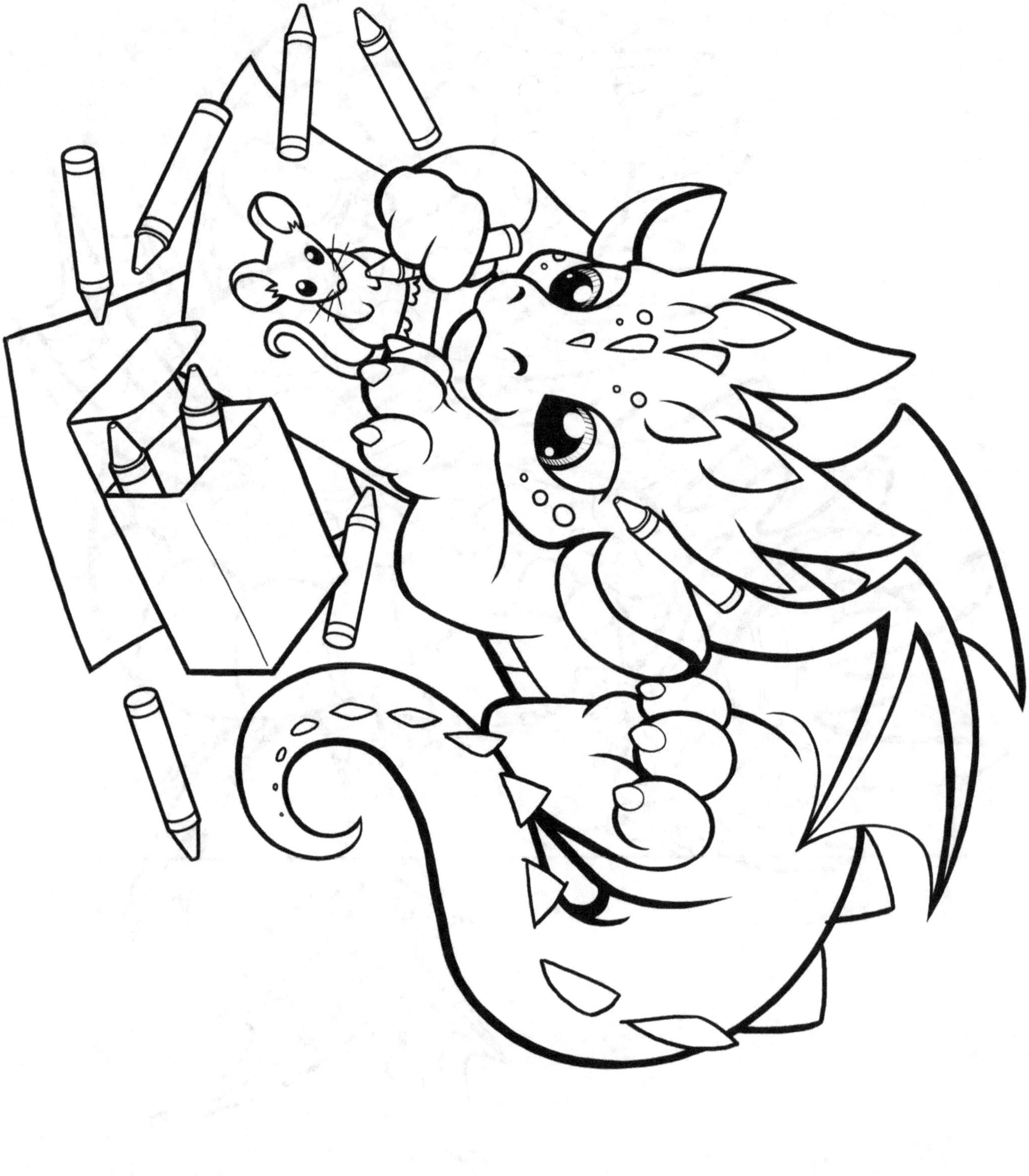

www.ingramcontent.com/pod-product-compliance
Lightning Source LLC
Chambersburg PA
CBHW080850170526
45158CB00009B/2694
* 9 7 8 0 6 9 2 3 4 0 9 1 2 *